"Go ye into all the world and preach the gospel to every creature."

"GO YE" MEANS YOU!

and other missionary messages
by Norman Lewis

INTRODUCTION
by Rev. Albert D. Helser, Ph.D.
General Director
Sudan Interior Mission

BACK TO THE BIBLE
Publication

50¢ EACH

order from

BACK TO THE BIBLE PUBLISHERS
BOX 233   LINCOLN 1, NEBR.

When you are finished with this book, why not pass it on to a friend?

INTRODUCTION

Make a Faith-Promise of your life to do the will of God. No one ever needs to be afraid of the will of God. His will for you is perfect. To do it will fill your soul with satisfaction and will give you a peace of God in your heart that passes all understanding. I made my Faith-Promise to do the will of God at any cost in 1916 when I was a freshman. That early morning of November 12th I set my face like a flint, and I kept it set through six more years of training, and on through forty wonderful years in Africa, and the best is yet ahead. Oh it is good to be committed to Christ for His cause, carrying the gospel around the world! This business is the greatest business in the world, and it pays a hundredfold. Yes, that is the sure promise of God—a hundredfold.

Norman Lewis saw the gleam and followed it to the blessing of Nebraska, the United States, South America, and the world. Norman faced up to the claim of Christ on his life as a student on October 21st, 1934, and surrendered his all to the Lord Jesus Christ. On a furlough from Africa I was speaking in Des Moines, Iowa, and I met this red-headed giant and loved him. Through the years, as both of us have gone all out to preach Christ "not where Christ was named" (Rom. 15:20), our fellowship has grown sweeter and sweeter.

In 1960, Brother Lewis wrote that wonderful book, "TRIUMPHANT MISSIONARY MINISTRY IN THE LOCAL CHURCH." It was published by The Good News Broadcasting Association, which circles the globe with the Good News—Jesus died to save sinners and Jesus died to save you. Norman is now Director of Missionary Conferences, and works night and day with those two missionary statesmen, Theodore H. Epp and G. Christian Weiss in Back to the Bible Broadcast, as it reaches to the ends of the earth, and at the same time does not forget the "Home Church" and individual saints and sinners.

The Sudan Interior Mission was so thrilled with Norman Lewis' book, "TRIUMPHANT MISSION-ARY MINISTRY IN THE LOCAL CHURCH," that we arranged for more than a thousand of our most interested, missionary-minded pastors to have copies. This book has blessed multitudes and has gone into its third printing. How happy I was to read the manuscript of Norman's new book, *"GO YE" MEANS YOU*.

As I read and thrilled, and read some more, my first burning thought was, "Oh, to be young again"; my second thought was, "This is God's call to the Church for this decade." The Holy Spirit filled our brother as he wrote, and as you read the Holy Spirit will fill you with a holy passion to finish the task God has commanded His disciples to finish. We must "preach the gospel to every creature." He has ordered it, and it shall be done.

On the way to a luncheon yesterday, I mentioned to a businessman that Norman Lewis has just written an important book. His quick comment was, "His letters, his articles, and his books, everything that man writes stirs me to the depths." As I read the manuscript the fires of God burned in my soul. I want you to heed these strong reasons from the Bible to go the limit for God now. Tomorrow will be too late.

—Albert D. Helser

CONTENTS

"GO YE" MEANS YOU

> "Go ye into all the world, and preach the gospel to
> every creature. He that believeth and is baptized
> shall be saved; but he that believeth not shall be
> damned" (Mark 16:15,16).

Every human being is implicated in the death
of Jesus Christ. Every last man will one day have
to face that fact. No one can elude that encounter.
Therefore, each of us does well to ask himself a
question. Pontius Pilate asked it long ago. "What
then shall I do with Jesus?" (Matt. 27:22).

So, too, every Christian is implicated in world
evangelization. Our Lord said, "Go ye into all the
world, and preach the gospel to every creature."
Each child of God is responsible to do his part. "Go
ye" means you. Every Christian will be judged at
last for his response to Christ's command.

Let it be plainly understood, however, that "Go
ye" is not chiefly a geographical command. Not
every Christian should be a missionary to a foreign
land. But every Christian should be willing to be
one. The question is commitment to Christ. He will
lead the committed Christian. It is His to decide
your field of service. The Lord of harvest will dis-

tribute His obedient children to evangelize the world. Abundant facts prove that this is the work of every Christian.

1. THIS IS WHAT GOD SAYS

This the Bible teaches. As Al Smith used to say, "Let's look at the record." Read the New Testament. The Gospels show in what terms the risen Christ laid the obligation of world evangelization upon His Church. Where do Christ's missionary commands occur? You will find them in the last chapters of Matthew, Mark, Luke, in John 17 and 20 and in the first chapter of Acts. "Go ye . . . make disciples among all nations." Again, "Go ye into all the world, and preach the gospel to every creature." Once more, "As my Father hath sent me, even so send I you." And yet again, "Ye shall be witnesses unto me . . . unto the uttermost part of the earth."

To these commands we must all respond. Nothing is said which would exclude any Christian. Each must share the task. Christ's word, "Ye are witnesses" is church-wide in application. It is world-wide in aim. That is what the Bible says. Logic compels it. A limited effort cannot get the gospel to every creature. The whole world can only be reached by Christ's whole army. God means you when He commands, "Go ye into all the world."

That fact was impressed upon me by an experience in Argentina. Christian nationals invited me for a tent campaign in Capilla del Senor. Evangelical meetings had never been held in the town. We began a street meeting. Many people gathered. Then a black Ford V-8 came charging up. It slammed to a stop. A black-robed figure jumped out. He hurried to a nearby police officer. We could not hear his words. But we saw his angry motions. He was telling the officer, "Stop them." The policeman refused. The priest stormed back to his car. He sat and glared at us. If looks could have killed, we would have died like flies.

Bible Proof

Later I greeted the man and offered him our evangelical paper, "La Voz." He refused it and said curtly, "If you want to talk with me, I live in the parochial house!" Next day I went with a national to call on the priest. We were invited into his study. My companion began to tell the reason for our meetings. We were simply obeying our Lord's command, "Go ye into all the world." The priest broke in. That word, he told us sharply, was for the apostles. It had nothing to do with those not in the apostolic succession. My mind wrestled with the problem. How could his argument be answered?

Then Acts 8 came to mind. I asked the priest whether he had a Bible. He took one down from an upper shelf. I asked him to read Acts 8:1. The verse describes a great persecution. It scattered the whole church "except the apostles." They remained at Jerusalem. Ordinary believers fled throughout Judea and Samaria. Then I asked him to read verse 4. "Therefore they that were scattered abroad [not apostles, but ordinary Christians] went every where preaching the word."

The priest was not slow of wit. He saw the point immediately. Without attempting an argument where none could be given, he turned to another subject. In spite of my attempts, he refused to return to Acts 8. These verses prove that world evangelization is the work of the whole church. God means you when He says, "Go ye into all the world, and preach the gospel."

2. GOD'S METHOD IS MEN

God might have sent angels to evangelize the world. But He did not. He might have broadcast the message from heaven. But He did not. He might have utilized a heavenly TV. But He did not. God chose to send men, men saved from sin, to win other sinners.

After His resurrection Christ ascended to heaven. He is pictured as being received with shouts of acclamation. Heaven's King re-entered the gates. He had voluntarily abandoned in order to go to earth and die. Someone has imagined Him being asked, "Lord, have you finished the work of redemption?"

He replied, "It is finished." Again heaven echoed with praise.

Then someone asked, "Lord, the world does not know. How will men find out?"

The Lord answered, "I have commanded Peter, James, John, and all my followers to go into the whole world and preach the gospel to every creature."

The questioner asked, "But Lord, what if they fail? What if Peter and John go back to fishing, and Matthew to tax collecting? What then?"

A shadow crossed the Lord's face as He said, "They must not fail. I have no other way." Christian, your Lord is counting on you.

Men Win Men

The whole New Testament shows saved sinners winning lost sinners. Think of Philip and the "man of Ethiopia" (Acts 8:27). The man was seeking God. In Jerusalem he had obtained a copy of the Scriptures. He was reading it. Yet when Philip asked him, "Do you clearly understand what you are reading?" he said, "How could I, unless some one guides me?" Then Philip, the saved sinner, led the lost sinner to Christ. This is God's way. His method is men.

The conversion of Paul is described in the next chapter. Perhaps it is unique. Certainly it is rare. God knocked Paul down. Yet even here God used men. For when Paul said, "Lord, what would you have me do?" God answered through Ananias. Ananias taught Paul.

A similar case follows in Acts 10. Cornelius is a praying man. So earnestly does he seek light that God sends an angel to him. Does the angel lead Cornelius to Christ? No. Oh, wonder of divine grace! Peter is the man who blasphemed on the night of Christ's betrayal. But now he leads Cornelius and his family to faith in Christ. God's goal is world evangelization. God's method is men.

Give to Win

God requires men for every phase of the work of global witness. Vast sums of money are needed. Every Christian should give. No gift is unimportant. The widow's mite is still great in the sight of God. The following letter is from a widow on a farm. Bitter waves of bereavement have rolled over her. She is the sole provider for eight children. A son lost an arm. But God . . . Her gifts to missions total $85.00 a month. She writes, "We are still praying for the Broadcast and all the workers in our family devotions. I am glad the children also feel the need to pray for you. I believe time is short for us to work. We need to be busy now in prayer, support, and labor. We will never be sorry for the little things we went without in order to keep ambassadors on the front lines."

That should be the focus of our giving. Many families could support their own missionary. Where the burden is too great for one family, let two or three families pool their gifts. Give to help finish the task.

3. THE CHURCH HAS FAILED FOR WANT OF WITNESSES

Almost two thousand years ago Christ commanded that the gospel be preached to every creature. Half the world is still unreached. Something is wrong. God is "not willing that any should perish" (II Pet. 3:9). Did God purpose a two thousand year delay in completing world evangelization? Surely not. Sixty generations have gone into a dark eternity. Millions of souls have died unreached. Who is to blame? Men, or God? This is an appalling problem. Dare we charge God? The cross proves His love. The Bible says, "God our Saviour . . . will have all men to be saved . . ." (I Tim. 2:3,4). Dare we blame God for the Church's failure?

God Has Called

G. Christian Weiss has declared, "I am convinced

that most Christians have missed the will of God for their lives." Every Christian should be deeply concerned. God commands that the gospel be preached to every creature. Has He not called enough Christians for the task? He must have. But the work has not been done. Why? Because Christians have disobeyed God's call.

"When I stand before the judgment throne
And see the unreached there
Shall I tell the Lord whose love I own
that I knew—but didn't care?"

What does it mean to you that half the world's population is unevangelized? What does it mean to you that there are more unreached people on earth than ever before? And they are increasing faster than we are telling them of Christ. Think this through. Something is rotten in Denmark. The Church's missionary outreach falls far short of minimum needs. Grim facts compel this conclusion. Some basic error must be present. An accusing finger points to Christians unwilling to obey God's command, "You go."

4. ALL OUT OF CHRIST ARE LOST

This is truth we do not like to face. It pains us. But the fact remains, men are lost. This made necessary God's plan of redemption. What brought God's Son to earth? He himself said, "The Son of man is come to seek and to save that which was lost" (Luke 19:10). The Bible teaches that by nature people are spiritually dead. All are dead to God. It is true whether men know the law of God or not. Paul says, "For as many as have sinned without law shall also perish without law" (Rom. 2:12). Out of Christ no human being can be saved. Someone says, "I cannot believe it. God is too loving and merciful to condemn eternally those who have never heard the gospel." Those words express an opinion. But this colossal matter will not be settled by opinions. Nor by feelings! Where God has spoken it is impertinence for men to offer their opinions.

Other Ways?

Imagine for a moment that the heathen could be saved without Christ. That would cut the vital nerve cord of missions. If men could be saved without our going to them, then why go? Why the sacrifice, separation, and suffering if the heathen are already heaven-bound? That supposition poses another problem. Wherever the gospel is preached it divides people. The same gospel is life unto life to those who receive Christ, and death unto death to those who reject. The same sun that melts the ice hardens the clay. The gospel itself means deeper damnation to men who hear and refuse it. Therefore, if men could be saved without Christ, we would do them no kindness to face them with the gospel.

This argument is valid. It shows how false is the idea that anyone can be saved without trusting Christ. The man who believes such a theory is pillowing his head upon a lie. All men out of Christ are lost. We must get the gospel to them at any cost. This is the solemn truth taught by God's Word.

Live Your Belief

Some years ago in England a condemned assassin, Charles Peace, was being led to the scaffold to die. At his side walked a clergyman speaking to him. After some time, Charles Peace suddenly said, "Do you really believe what you have just been telling me?"

"Certainly, I do," said the clergyman, a bit shaken by the vehemence of the question.

"No you don't," said Peace with a hard tone. "If I believed what you say you believe, I would crawl across England on my hands and knees over fields strewn with broken glass to tell men and women about it. You don't believe it yourself!"

Maybe Peace was not far wrong. Could men point the finger at you and say, "You don't believe it yourself?" Lost millions at the judgment may charge us with their doom. Their salvation depends upon our faithfulness. God means you when He says, "Go ye." Commitment to Christ for world evangelization is the only answer. No other solution will meet the world's needs. Remember, God will not ask what you cannot do. But what you can do, you must. God asks you to give yourself to Him. Do that. Claim His promised guidance. Help reach every creature with the gospel. God does mean you.

MISSIONARY PREACHING AND PURPOSE

> "All things must be fulfilled, which were written in the law of Moses, and in the prophets, and in the psalms, concerning me. Then opened he their understanding, that they might understand the Scriptures, And said unto them, Thus it is written, and thus it behooved Christ to suffer, and to rise from the dead the third day: And that repentance and remission of sins should be preached in his name among all nations beginning at Jerusalem" (Luke 24:44-47).

A Christian uninformed of missions is like an aviator without a plane or a farmer without a farm. Missions is a must for every Christian. "Is that true?" you may ask. How can we find out? No one qualifies like Jesus Christ to explain God's missionary enterprise. Christ appears on the evening of the first Lord's day. He asks for food, eats before the disciples and begins to speak. Amazing words are uttered with artless simplicity.

In God's Plan

First, Christ declares world evangelization to be part of God's primitive plan. The coming missionary enterprise is contemplated in earlier revelation. Jesus says, "All things must be fulfilled, which were written . . ." World evangelization in the Old Testament? Yes. Any doubt as to this is removed by Christ's further words. "Thus it is written . . . that repentance and remission of sins should be preached in his name among all nations." Jesus declares that God's plan to evangelize the nations is recorded in the Old Testament Scriptures. This is indeed significant. World evangelization is no afterthought on the part of God. It is not an emergency plan. Nor is it a sudden scheme devised by God due to the alteration of some previous purpose. The missionary enterprise in the New Testament pours forth like a great river. Its upper headwaters flow from Old Testament revelation.

Second, notice what follows: "Then opened he their understanding, that they might understand the scriptures." How noteworthy this is! A Christ-quickened understanding was needed if men were to comprehend the missionary enterprise. It was true then, it is just as true today. How many of God's children live with eyes veiled to the primacy of world evangelization. Oh that our Lord might enlighten the eyes of our understanding! Only thus will we see clearly the great task He has left us to do.

Our Lord now describes the task to be done. In briefest words He defines the whole missionary enterprise, its preaching, its purpose, its personnel, and its power.

1. ITS PREACHING: CHRIST

Our Lord places Himself as the center and theme of the preaching that is to accomplish world evangelization (Luke 24:46,47a). He does so deliberately. Christ's attitude sets Him apart from all mere human leaders. With neither reticence nor bombast our Lord recognizes His inevitable pre-eminence. Our message is Christ.

What Christ must we preach? The suffering, dying One? I had not been a month in Argentina in 1945 when I made my first trip into the interior. While traveling we suddenly came upon a shrine. On a cross hung an almost full-sized figure of the dying Saviour. Quickly we took in the details: the distorted face, twisted limbs, hideous wounds with their painted blood. That figure, I realized aghast, was the only Saviour millions of sinful men know. There He hangs, forever on nails, a dying victim, devoid of power to heal, or help, or save. Mark it well. This religion comes not from above. This is but an imitation of true Christianity. But it is fashioned with consummate skill. How clever Satan is! How well he has learned his work. He gives men a caricature of the truth. That generally makes them forever immune to the real thing.

Risen

What Christ must we preach? Notice carefully. Our Lord presents together His dying and rising. Nothing must cause men to think of the dying Saviour apart from the living Saviour. From Pentecost onward the apostles blazed abroad the message of a crucified, risen Saviour. The resurrection was a vital ingredient in the gospel bread the early church gave out. In Athens Paul preached Jesus and the resurrection. Some philosophers got mixed up. They thought Paul was presenting a plurality of gods "because he preached unto them Jesus, and the resurrection" (Acts 17:18). The Apostle John on Patmos heard Christ say, "I am he that liveth, and was dead;

and, behold, I am alive forevermore, Amen" (Rev. 1:18).

Conqueror

What Christ is to be preached? The living Christ, King of kings and Lord of lords. His perfect holiness and hatred for sin make necessary God's command—repent. We are to preach repentance in His name. Christ once humbled Himself in voluntary obedience to the death of the cross. "Wherefore God also hath highly exalted him, and given him a name which is above every name: That at the name of Jesus every knee should bow, of things in heaven, and things in earth, and things under the earth; And that every tongue should confess that Jesus Christ is Lord, to the glory of God the Father" (Phil. 2:9-11).

Men Repent

Peter was deeply gripped by this truth. See him preach to the vast crowd at Pentecost. Before him are men whose hands are red with the blood of God's Son. Peter says of Christ, "Him . . . ye have taken, and by wicked hands have crucified and slain" (Acts 2:23). This is the suffering Christ. "Whom God hath raised up" (2:24). And again, "This Jesus hath God raised up" (2:32). This is the risen Christ.

But Peter must yet more exalt his Lord and humble human pride. At last he says, "Therefore let all the house of Israel know assuredly, that God hath made that same Jesus, whom ye have crucified, both Lord and Christ" (2:36). This is Christ the Lord. His fear struck those hearts. Three thousand men cried out, "What shall we do?" Peter replied, "Repent and be baptized every one of you in the name of Jesus Christ for the remission of sins . . ." Men of any race, anywhere, who repent and obey Christ will be pardoned. This is the message God has ordered us to give all men.

2. ITS PURPOSE: WORLD-WIDE WITNESS

The purpose of the missionary enterprise is closely related to the preaching and stems from it (Luke 24:27b). In all the world men must repent. Then to all the world must the message be sent. The scope of the enterprise is world-wide. Here and elsewhere we read the clear-cut phrases, "among all nations . . . unto the uttermost part of the earth . . . to every creature." The Revelation shows us the throne of the Lamb of God surrounded by those His blood has redeemed. Included there are men from "every kindred, and tongue, and people, and nation" (Rev. 5:9). This is God's prophetic promise. This is God's goal. Someone asks, "Can I be sure what God's purpose is?" You can. "It is written." The missionary enterprise, like a mammoth building, rests on Bible bedrock. Years ago I determined to settle this question for myself. I read the New Testament deliberately to find out what it said about God's purpose. I wanted to see whether God had a plan. With what results?

The Vital Theme

In Matthew I read Jesus' command, "Go . . . make disciples of all nations" (Matt. 28:19). In Mark His word was, "Go ye into all the world, and preach the gospel to every creature" (Mark 16:15). In Luke our text met me, "Repentance and remission of sins should be preached in his name among all nations." Nor was John less plain, "Then said Jesus . . . as my Father hath sent me, even so send I you" (John 20:21).

Acts brought the familiar words, "Ye shall be witnesses unto me . . . unto the uttermost part of the earth" (Acts 1:8). I attended the church council at Jerusalem and listened as Simeon "declared how God at first did visit the Gentiles, to take out of them a people for his name" (15:14). In Romans I heard Paul say, "Whosoever shall call upon the name of the Lord shall be saved. How then shall they call on him in whom they have not believed? and how shall they believe in him of whom they have not heard? and how shall they hear without a preacher? And how shall they preach, except they be sent?" (Rom. 10:13-15).

Revelation sums up the whole program. "They sung a new song, saying, Thou art worthy . . . for thou wast slain, and hast redeemed us to God by thy blood out of every kindred, and tongue, and people, and nations" (Rev. 5:9). The throbbing, vital core of New Testament redemption is the Church's responsibility to evangelize the whole, wide world. The Bible reveals God's purpose in our age. No one need be ignorant of it.

Read It Yourself

Permit a word of warning. Read the Bible for yourself. Dig into it. You may think that listening to a preacher is the same as reading the Bible. Look out! An experience in Argentina comes to mind. Buenos Aires is one of the world's largest cities. Our first home there was an apartment in a residential section. One day I heard the sound of cowbells. We went to the door. Sure enough, down the paved street a half dozen gaunt cows were being herded. The driver halted them before a neighbor's house. A woman walked out and handed the man a pitcher. He squatted down on his heels and proceeded to milk into the pitcher. I was puzzled. Why didn't he milk the cows in the country and bring only the milk to town?

"Oh no—a neighbor told me—this way is much better. This is milk at the foot of the cow. Milk bought in cans may be watered down. When you buy milk at the foot of the cow you get pure milk!" Likewise, read the Bible for yourself. Where God's Word is concerned, "Milk at the foot of the cow" is the best rule. The Apostle Peter said, "As newborn babes, desire the sincere milk of the word" (I Pet. 2:2). You have one life to invest. Be sure you know God's purpose. Find it yourself from the Bible.

What Progress?

God's goal is world evangelization. What progress has the Church made toward that goal? "A great deal," you may say. True. Yet, a closer study is disturbing. We face startling facts. At least one-half the world's population is still unevangelized. Do you know there are more unreached people today than when Christ first gave the missionary command? And the unevangelized increase faster than we are reaching them with the gospel. In terms of Christ's miracle when He fed the hungry multitude, we are feeding only the front rows. The back rows starve. In a few favored lands the bread of life is offered through churches, by radio, television, the printed page. Yonder the expanding millions die with gospel crumbs.

Anchored?

But God is moving toward those unevangelized millions. Are you going God's way? Many Christians have no world vision. They are rooted. Lines learned in college days come to mind:

"Fixed like a plant to his peculiar spot
to draw nutrition, propagate, and rot."

Like the drunk who staggered out of the water front tavern one night and got into his boat to row across the river. Hour after hour he pulled at the oars. "Funny," he said, "I don't seem to be making much progress." Still he rowed. When morning came he found the trouble. His boat was anchored. Many church people have a similar problem. Their talk about world evangelization means little for they are anchored. Anchored to a job, anchored to a beautiful home, anchored to a circle of friends!

Be Wise!

God is on the march! Our place is with Him. Paul says, "Be ye not unwise, but understanding what the will of the Lord is" (Eph. 5:17). The Christian who rejects his part in God's world task limits himself to trifles. He is merely making daisy chains. The man unrelated to world evangelization is cutting out paper dolls. Nothing more! Much of what men call great is an abomination in the sight of God. Oh the curse of inconsequential living! To pay lip service to missions, and live for other things, is folly. Do not cross the current of God's will.

During high school days I spent two months in the high rockies. Our camp was near Berthoud Pass, at some 8,000 feet of altitude. One day I was trout fishing along the river. The far bank promised better fishing. But rushing, icy water had to be crossed. And there was no bridge. Finally a place appeared where the river widened. I tried to wade across. All went well until I neared the other bank. Suddenly I stepped into deep water. Quicker than I can tell it I was swept off my feet. The icy water slammed me along head over heels. My plight was desperate. A hundred yards or more down stream I grabbed a friendly tree root. Half drowned I dragged myself ashore. To try to cross that current was a mistake. The current of God's will moves toward world evangelization. Move with God.

MISSIONARY PERSONNEL AND POWER

"Ye are witnesses of these things. And, behold, I send the promise of my Father upon you: but tarry ye in the city of Jerusalem, until ye be endued with power from on high" (Luke 24:48,49).

A Christian unrelated to world evangelization is a pathetic and futile figure. His time is taken up with trifles. He is like a fish out of water. He is not in his true element. As we have already seen, basic missionary preaching and purpose is set forth in Luke 24:44-47. God "commands all men everywhere to repent" (Acts 17:30). Therefore, men everywhere must be introduced to Jesus Christ. This is God's plan. Personnel and power also figure in the divine blue print of missions. Let us consider:

1. ITS PERSONNEL: "YOU"

"Ye are witnesses of these things" (v. 48). You, Christian, are needed for world evangelization. This is perhaps the chief reason God did not take you home to heaven as soon as you had made your decision for Christ. Heaven is a wonderful place. The most spiritual men ever to walk the face of God's green earth have longed and desired to enter that fair land. Only the fact that we are such earth-bound clods makes us want to remain here. The Apostle Paul desired to depart and be with Christ which he said "is far better." God could remove every child of His from this vale of tears as soon as Christ had been received in the heart. Why does He not do so?

Our Task

One reason is plain. There is a job to be done. God has made us His ambassadors. The fate of millions of lost men hangs upon our faithfulness. Who can measure the meaning of such a statement? Much as we might wish to change these facts, the Bible is plain. God says, "When I say unto the wicked, Thou shalt surely die; and thou givest him not warning, nor speakest to warn the wicked from his wicked way, to save his life; the same wicked man shall die in his iniquity . . ." (Ezek. 3:18). Ignorance will not save. Paul states, "As many as have sinned without law shall also perish without law . . ." (Rom. 2:12). Peter declares, "There is none other name under heaven given among men, whereby we must be saved" (Acts 4:12). Jesus Christ himself says, "No man cometh unto the Father, but by me" (John 14:6). We must tell all men of Christ! What a solemn thing it is to be a Christian.

In Our Generation

This generation of Christians must reach this generation of unevangelized persons. For them, there is no other way to God. Surely common sense assists us here. God will not hold us responsible for the unevangelized souls who perished before our time. Nor can we answer for the souls that may be born after we die. But to our own generation we drinketh of this water shall thirst again; But ever drinketh of the water that I shall give all never thirst; but the water that I shall m shall be in him a well of water springing o everlasting life" (vv. 13,14). Jesus is evident-aking of the gift of the indwelling Holy Spirit. s becomes apparent from His statement made e last great day of the feast. He said, "If any thirst, let him come unto me, and drink. He believeth on me, as the scripture hath said, out s belly shall flow rivers of living water. (But spake he of the Spirit, which they that believe im should receive: for the Holy Ghost was not given; because that Jesus was not yet glorified" n 7:37-39).

After this Jesus was crucified, buried, raised from dead. He then spoke the words of our text: nd, behold, I send the promise of my Father upon u: but tarry ye in the city of Jerusalem, until ye endued with power from on high" (Luke 24:49). the opening verses of the Book of Acts, Luke re-ers again to this promise. He gives the words of esus: "Wait for the promise of the Father" as well s his further words: "Ye shall be baptized with the Holy Ghost not many days hence" (Acts 1:4,5).

Power for Us

The coming of the Holy Spirit as recorded in Acts 2 is well known. The significant fact is that power for world evangelization had been promised by the Son of God. That promise was fulfilled in the com-ing of the Holy Spirit at Pentecost. It is needful to remember how far that promise reaches. When Peter called men to repentance and baptism in the

34

can and must be true. If we fail here, our failure will be complete. We read that David, "after he had served his own generation by the will of God, fell on sleep" (Acts 13:36). David's life span was his only opportunity to serve his generation. If he had failed there, nothing could have righted the awful wrong committed. How good it is that David did not fail. He served his own generation by the will of God. Christian, when the recording angel writes your name down at the close of your life's little day, will the inscription be the same? God help you to be true.

The Key Is Men

The shortage is men. The task is great, but com-mitted men are few. Our Lord faced this problem long ago. "When He saw the crowds, His heart was moved with pity for them, because they were tired and scattered like sheep without a shepherd. Then He said to His disciples, The harvest is plentiful, but the reapers are scarce. So pray the Lord of the harvest to send out reapers to His harvest field" (Matt. 9:36,38, Williams).

The truth has been well put by E. M. Bounds. He says, "We are constantly straining to devise new methods, new plans, new organizations to advance the Church and secure enlargement and efficiency for the gospel. This trend of the day has a tendency to lose sight of the man or sink the man in the plan or organization. God's plan is to make much of the man, far more of him than of anything else. Men are God's method.

"The Church is looking for better methods; God is looking for better men. 'There was a man sent from God whose name was John.' The dispensation that heralded and prepared the way for Christ was bound up in that man John.

" 'Unto us a child is born, unto us a Son is given.' The world's salvation comes out of that cradled Son. When Paul appeals to the personal character of the men who rooted the gospel in the world, he solves the mystery of their success. The glory and efficiency of the gospel are staked on the men who proclaim it. When God declares that 'the eyes of the Lord run to and fro throughout the whole earth, to show Himself strong in the behalf of them whose heart is perfect toward Him,' He declares the necessity of men and His dependence on them as a channel through which to exert His power upon the world."

A Personal Issue

Christian, you must face this. God commands you. He is counting on you to get the gospel to souls still unreached. What will your answer be? It is not an easy decision. Let me tell you without apology the experience of the man I know best.

Soon after I was saved, I learned the primacy of missions. Splendid missionaries visited our church. Noble men and women! How they inspired and challenged us. Was my life offered for missionary service? No, with shame it must be said. Other plans had first place. I was a graduate of the University of Nebraska and engaged to be married. On Cotner Boulevard a wooded lot had been chosen as a home site. Missions? Oh yes. One wing of the house was to be used for the entertainment of tired missionaries home on furlough. That was to be my

contribution to world evan

But God would not ha
heavens brass above me an
my prayers. Finally, in miser
heart and told her we would h
gagement because I was going
issue was that of full surrende
be settled in my life. It must k
of every Christian. Later, Go
marry the same girl, and we
missionary service in Central Asia
delay due to war, and with doors t
we went to South America. There
fourteen wonderful years of missior

Christian, you are part of God',
the missionary enterprise. Your fu.
Him is prerequisite to knowing His
life. You will not be handed your pe
marching orders, until you have volur.
you declare yourself expendable? The
then, will God show you what to do.

2. ITS POWER: THE HOLY SPI

Power for world evangelization is prom.
hold I send the promise of my Father u.
(v. 49). This is the statement of the Son of
deserves our careful consideration. This is
nary promise. It is vast, basic, and vital. Ou
unfolded it carefully during His ministry. Jes
to the Samaritan woman at the well, "If thou
est the gift of God, and who it is that saith to
Give me to drink; thou wouldest have asked of
and he would have given thee living water" (J
4:10). Jesus further explained to the woman, "W

name of Jesus he said, "And ye shall receive the gift of the Holy Ghost. For the promise is unto you, and to your children, and to all that are afar off, even as many as the Lord our God shall call" (Acts 2:38,39). The promise Christ had made was plainly, literally fulfilled. It was plainly declared valid for every believer to the present hour.

Why This Power?

Let us pause and contemplate the task Christ assigned His followers. He said, "Preach the gospel to every creature." Never before had such an order been given. All men everywhere must be introduced to Jesus Christ. Is the work difficult? Indeed it is. Let the whole truth be stated. By all human standards the task seems not only difficult, but impossible. To attempt such an enterprise with human energy could only spell failure. Therefore, Christ strongly warns His disciples against false confidence or too hasty beginnings. The work can only be done with the power God provides. But the fact remains, God has commanded us to evangelize the world. And when God commands, He equips. "Ye shall receive power, after that the Holy Ghost is come upon you" (Acts 1:8).

Power in a Person

Power in a Person has been given. The Spirit of God is here now. He has come. He dwells within every child of God. If you are a Christian, you have Him.

Dr. Timothy Richard asked a Chinese philanthropist, not a Christian, if he had read the New Testament. "Three times," he answered. "And what impressed you most?" the doctor asked. After a pause the man said, "I think the most wonderful thing to me in the whole Bible is this, that it is possible for men to become temples of the Holy Ghost." The meaning of this tremendous truth escapes human measure.

Someone once said to Evan Roberts, "We have not power enough." Mr. Roberts answered, "My brother, power is a Person, and we have got the Holy Ghost."

Does He Have You?

It is sadly possible for a Christian to have the Holy Spirit and yet be unsurrendered to God. Christian, you have the Holy Spirit. Does He have you? All of you? Does the Holy Spirit rule and reign in every area of your personality? That is the question. The Spirit who kissed cold clay into life on creation's morning has still His ancient power. But each human will can limit or let loose that power. Oh let us not hinder the Holy Spirit! May He breathe life through us to lost souls among every kindred, tongue, people and nation. This must be our aim till Jesus Christ comes back again.

Ashes Only

Last furlough, I sat one morning in my car beside a lake at a Minnesota resort. Thoughts of world evangelization were running through my mind. A few feet away stood a large metal container bearing the words, "Ashes Only." It simply meant the barrel was to be used for ashes. But as I meditated, those words took on a larger meaning. I saw they applied to everything we have that is not vitally connected with world evangelization. Christian, take that phrase with you from this hour. Write "Ashes Only" on your dearest possessions. Write those words on your house, your car, your best clothes, your sports equipment, your checkbook, your insurance policy, your stocks and bonds. Write them across the name of your sweetheart, your wife, your husband, your children. All these things that men hold dear are worth nothing if not surrendered to God for the task of world evangelization. Let us boldly face this vital truth and dare to obey.

FACTS WE MUST FACE

"Go ye into all the world, and preach the gospel
to every creature" (Mark 16:15).
"Why call ye me, Lord, Lord, and do not the things
which I say?" (Luke 6:46).
"We ought to obey God" (Acts 5:29).

To evangelize the world is the most significant
business on earth. "Why is that?" you may say. Because of its main motive.

1. CHRIST COMMANDED IT

Suppose you and I had gone to Christ's tomb on
the resurrection morning. Our hearts are sad and
full of gloom. We see the stone rolled away. We go
into the tomb. There a young man says to us, "You
must not be so astounded; you are looking for Jesus
of Nazareth who was crucified. He has risen; He is
not here. See! here is the spot where they laid Him.
But you go and tell His disciples and Peter, 'He is
going back to Galilee to meet you; you will see Him
there, just as He told you!' " We go to Galilee. Christ
appears and says, "Go ye into all the world, and
preach the gospel to every creature."

That is the basis for missions. It is not a challenge. This is a command. The words challenge and
command are similar. Yet their meaning is not the
same. A challenge is an invitation to engage in a

contest. It may be a summons to fight, as a duel. One is challenged when called defiantly to a contest. In such a case there may be reasons to accept or good grounds to refuse. You are challenged to do something. You decide it is best not to do so. You say "no." There the matter ends. A command is different. The word command means to direct authoritatively. The very idea of a command is that of an order given by someone who has a right to give it. Therefore, the word command suggests an official exercise of authority.

His Right

The Lord Jesus has every right to command His followers. We belong to Him, body, soul and spirit. Christ owns us by right of creation. And He owns us by right of redemption. No child of God can honorably deny the Lordship of Christ in His life. At least that is what we Christians think we believe. What about our practice?

The Duke of Wellington was an able military man. A Christian once asked him what he thought about the possibility of carrying out the great commission. The Duke replied sharply, "What are your orders, sir?" He was too much a soldier to quibble about obedience to a command. A command issued by a man who has the right to give it must be obeyed. This is true of the Christian. His one right attitude is that of active obedience to Jesus Christ.

A Clear Command

This command is plain. "You go!" These words make every Christian responsible for world evangelization. Some Christians object they are waiting for a call. But the call "is written." The Bible gives it in black and white. It answers the question each Christian naturally asks, "Lord, what wilt thou have me to do?" (Acts 9:6). God's call reveals God's purpose. Many Christians suppose they should "feel" a call to foreign service. A bit of reflection will show us how natural that is. By nature we prefer our own locality and people. We naturally like our own customs and land. But our relation to Christ is supernatural. And the Christian is made a missionary by his relation to Christ. Christ's command, "Go ye" is clear. The burden of proof rests upon anyone who answers that command with less than outright obedience.

Years ago I heard the thrilling testimony of a missionary who had spent more than fifty years in the Congo. His half century of missionary service had been rich and fruitful. He told us he had not been conscious of a special, inward missionary call. He had simply read Christ's plain command, "You go." He knew a Christian should obey. He committed himself to Christ, made preparation and went to dark Africa. A long, useful missionary career followed. He obeyed God.

Last Words

The last command Christ gave was to evangelize the world. Our risen Lord commanded His followers to be witnesses for Him to the uttermost part of the earth. The Bible says, "And when he had spoken these things, while they beheld, he was taken up; and a cloud received him out of their sight" (Acts 1:9).

I never knew my grandfather Lewis. He died before I was born. His was a hard pioneer life. When grandfather fell sick the last time, my father was teaching school far away. When he received the news of the serious illness he started home. It was mid-winter. He arrived at the little town of Butternut, Michigan. Heavy snow lay on the ground. He started hiking down the railroad track taking a shortcut to the farm home. A handcar came along. The men picked him up. They were neighbors. Dad asked, "Have you heard any word about my father?" There was silence. Then a man said, "He is dead."

As father neared the house, his sister rushed to meet him. They embraced, both were weeping. Father asked, "Did he leave any message for me?" His sister said, "Yes, he did. When he knew that he was going he said, 'It is better this way. He will remember me as I was.' Then he said, 'Tell Glen always to live true to Jesus.' With that he was gone." Could my father ever forget those last words? When he told them to me he said, "Norman, that was 40 years ago, but I remember it as though it were yesterday." Precious words! They were the last utterance of a loved one. Christ ordered us to witness for Him, "To the uttermost part of the earth." Consider those last words of His. What place do they have in your heart?

2. WE HAVE NOT OBEYED

What if the Lord Jesus should suddenly appear and say to us, "Why call ye me, Lord, Lord, and do not the things which I say"? What could we answer? History shows the root of the Church's disobedience. Acts 8 tells of the man from Ethiopia. He was one of the earliest African converts to Christianity. In the dawn of the Christian era the gospel gained a foothold in north Africa. Strong churches developed. Progress was great. More than a quarter of the whole number of churches in Christendom were soon to be found there. In the third and fourth centuries after Christ there were more Christians there than in any other area. The north African church produced great theologians—Augustine, Cyprian, Origen, and Tertullian. Did the church obey God and carry the gospel to the rest of Africa? The sad answer is, "no." Those Christians forgot their main reason for being. The churches weakened, dwindled, and finally succumbed to the Moslem advance. And vital Christianity disappeared from Africa. The solemn fact is that during 1,500 years of the Church's history, the missionary emphasis was conspicuous by its absence.

What Fruits?

If history shows the root of disobedience, present statistics show its fruit. Half the world is unreached for Christ. Unevangelized masses increase faster than we give to them the gospel. The way we spend our money shows how little we care for Christ's command. The average American spends more on chewing gum each year than the average member of two of the largest denominations gives for missions. How do you use your money? How much do you spend on cokes, cosmetics, sporting equipment and show going, your car, your clothes, your home, your hobby? Our Lord's question goes deep. What part of the money you spend carries the gospel to unreached men?

Church budgets reveal our disobedience to Christ's missionary command. For the last two years an average of a billion dollars a year has been spent in the United States for new churches or religious buildings. For this we spend more than two and a half million dollars a day! Remember, we have been put in trust with the gospel. Souls without number sit in the darkness and shadow of death. They cannot wait long years for us to pay off church building debts before we give to missions.

Blindness

We have removed world evangelization from its central place in the New Testament. This affects our whole interpretation of the Bible. We emphasize texts which console and comfort us. Christ's burning commands are set aside. Sermons stress believing more than doing, our blessings rather than our obedience.

G. Christian Weiss shared a conference with a nationally known Bible teacher. They met together before the service. The Bible teacher prayed, "Dear Lord, help our brother as he carries the missionary end of the conference."

After the prayer Mr. Weiss asked the man whether he really meant just what he had prayed. "Do you not feel that you too share the missionary responsibility?" he asked.

Said the famous conference speaker, "I am a Bible teacher." Mr. Weiss insisted that the missionary responsibility belongs to every Christian. The Bible teacher only said, "I must confess I never thought much about it."

Surely such a man is a "blind leader." How can

anyone teach the Bible and leave out missions? Beginning in the Gospels the whole thrust of the New Testament is the Church's responsibility to evangelize the world. How pointless the Bible becomes if that fact is ignored!

3. "WE MUST OBEY GOD"

That is what the apostle said in an hour of crisis. The prophet of old said, "To obey is better than sacrifice." Thank God for men who have obeyed. They put missions in first place. Dr. A. B. Simpson founded the Christian and Missionary Alliance, one of the great missionary movements of our day. Dr. Simpson was a spiritual giant. His influence reached around the world. One morning a friend who was staying in his home walked by Dr. Simpson's study. The door stood ajar. The friend glanced in. Dr. Simpson stood beside the desk praying. His hands rested on a globe of the world. As he prayed he wept. His falling tears wet the globe as his heart's cry went up to God for the lost of earth. The astonished visitor felt he had glimpsed the secret of the mighty missionary outreach of the movement led by Dr. Simpson.

God gives us hearts like that!

God gives priority to missions. Therefore, every Christian ought to spend more on missions than on all else. Every church should do the same. Some churches do. They spend more each year on foreign missions than on all local expenses. Such churches are a small minority. Their number, however, is increasing. The proportion of a church's income which is spent on missions is a measure of its love for Christ.

A Decisive Commitment

To live thus demands a decisive commitment. The Apostle Paul said, "I beseech you therefore, brethren, by the mercies of God, that ye present your bodies . . ." (Rom. 12:1). Are you willing to surrender your life to God to reach a lost world? This is the practical issue.

A negro youth in Africa understood. A Thanksgiving offering was being received in the grass roofed church. The Christians passed forward in a file. Some brought fruit, others vegetables, a chicken, eggs, or similar produce. Each placed his offering at the front. The young man remained at the rear of the church. His heart was broken. He had no offering to bring. But he loved his Lord. Then he picked up a small empty basket and went forward. He put the basket down among the other offerings and stepped into it. There he stood for a few moments with hands folded and eyes closed. Then he returned to his place at the rear of the church.

Afterward the missionary spoke to the boy. "It was beautiful, what you did," he said, "but just what did you mean by it?"

The youth said, "When others were taking their gifts I was sad because I had nothing to give. Then I remembered I could give myself. When I stood in the basket I told God I was giving myself to preach the gospel or do whatever He wants me to do." Have you stood in the basket? Have you given yourself away to Jesus Christ?

This results from decisive commitment. Romans 12:2 describes an inward transformation. The committed Christian has a renewed mind. He has new ideals and new attitudes. His thinking is in harmony with God's plan for world evangelization. The same text shows that the yielded Christian will be led into the will of God for his life. God's general will is world evangelization. God's special will for each life is revealed on the basis of personal commitment to Christ.

Keep your life on the altar. Taylor Smith was a great power for God. He once revealed to a friend a prayer he often prayed. He said that before he even got out of bed in the morning he would say, "Oh God, make this bed on which I rest an altar and my body reclining on it a sacrifice. In the teaching of Romans 12:1, I present it to you again this morning, a living sacrifice." This is a practical prayer. Christian, keep your life on the altar for Christ.

A missionary party outward bound for the Pacific Islands was ridiculed by the ship's captain. The scoffer said, "You will only die out there." A missionary answered, "We died before we started." This death to self-will is the royal road of obedience. Those who walk that road will know and do the will of God. "We must obey God."

OBEDIENCE AND WORLD MISSIONS

"We must obey God" (Acts 5:29, A.S.V.).

World evangelization is a vast enterprise. It should be examined from many angles. Each viewpoint offers particular advantages. We are now concerned with world missions from the standpoint of obedience.

1. CHRIST DID COMMAND HIS CHURCH TO EVANGELIZE THE WORLD

Forty days the risen Christ met with His followers before His ascension. His emphasis during that time was world evangelization. Christ's great commission is not vague. The first Gospel gives these words, "All power is given unto me in heaven and in earth. Go ye therefore, and teach all nations" (Matt. 28:18,19). The command in Mark is very personal, "Go ye into all the world, and preach the gospel to every creature" (Mark 16:15). A wealth of detail accompanies the command in the last chapter of Luke. Twice it is stated in the closing chapters of John and again in Acts 1:8. Why this repetition? Because Christ's command is supremely important.

The Bible describes the Church as a militant army. Jesus Christ is called the Captain of our salvation. In the Revelation He is seen as Rider of a white horse followed by the heavenly armies. Just before His crucifixion He said to His followers, "Ye call me Master and Lord: and ye say well; for so I am" (John 13:13). The Son of God did not cloak Himself with false modesty. He was bold and forthright to assert His authority. His claims on us are absolute.

Every Christian is a soldier. "Thou therefore endure hardness, as a good soldier of Jesus Christ" (II Tim. 2:3). Paul says to the Ephesians, "Put on the whole armour of God" (Eph. 6:11). And again to Timothy, "Fight the good fight of faith" (I Tim. 6:12). For a soldier to refuse obedience to an officer's command is insubordination. It is not tolerated in any army. Woe to the Christian who merits Christ's rebuke, "Why call ye me, Lord, Lord, and do not the things which I say?" (Luke 6:46).

It boils down to this. Our Captain has commanded us to evangelize the world. No one denies the order has been given. No one questions Christ's right to give it. Are we obedient soldiers? Or are we the chocolate kind, sweet and soft, and artificial? Refusal is sin. Not to obey is to disobey.

The Rothschilds were famous financiers. They exacted unqualified obedience from their employees. A story illustrates the fact. They once had an alert young agent in New Orleans. The New York office wired him to sell their cotton holdings on a certain date. The agent believed the price of cotton was going up. He delayed the sale four days. An extra profit resulted. The young agent sent the Rothschilds a check in full and explained what he had done. Back came a check for the extra amount with a cold note that said, "The money you made disobeying our orders is yours, not ours. Take it. Your successor sails for New Orleans today." The man was fired!

The Rothschilds would not have a man on their staff who would disobey a plain order. What about us? Have we thought how serious it is for a Christian to disobey God?

2. OBEDIENCE, THE ISSUE

Obedience is basic to man's relation to God. This is an old question. It has been a chief issue since creation's morning. God placed man in a perfect environment. Only one prohibition limited his freedom. "Do not eat from the tree of the knowledge of good and evil" (Gen. 2:17). That was necessary to test man's obedience. But Adam and Eve disobeyed God. That was their sin. For that they were cast out of Eden. That sin brought God's curse upon the earth. All the misery and heartache that has blighted the earth to the present moment stems from this same sin.

The tendency to disobedience is deeply rooted in us all. Adam's sin in Eden suggests this sin might crop up again and again in human history. That is just what occurs. The Bible accounts of Cain, Achan, and Saul give prominence to the sin of disobedience. The Bible also tells of men who obeyed. There was Enoch who "walked with God." Noah obeyed God and preached righteousness for 120 years. Caleb and Joshua were obedient. Caleb "wholly followed the Lord his God."

The Apostle Peter said, "We must obey God." Paul testified, "I was not disobedient unto the heavenly vision." Our Lord is the supreme example of perfect obedience. Jesus could say of His walk before God, "I do always those things which please him" (John 8:29). "Though he were a Son, yet learned he obedience by the things which he suffered" (Heb. 5:8). He became "obedient unto death, even the death of the cross" (Phil. 2:8).

3. OBEDIENCE, DECISIVE

How much does obedience matter? Notice:

Human redemption hinged on Christ's obedience to God. If Jesus Christ had disobeyed God, there could have been no cross and no redemption for mankind. The atonement depended on Christ's obedience. He did not turn aside but became "obedient unto death."

Hope for the heathen hinges on our obedience to God. Heaven or hell are in the issue. God's Word says of all men, "He that believeth not is condemned already" (John 3:18). Christ commands us to preach the gospel to every creature. But He also declares, "He that believeth not shall be damned" (Mark 16:16). The Apostle Paul teaches that men can be saved only by calling upon the name of the Lord. His theology holds no hint of any other way. He says, "How then shall they call on him in whom they have not believed? and how shall they believe in him of whom they have not heard? and how shall they hear without a preacher? And how shall they preach, except they be sent?" (Rom. 10:14,15). The Bible declares there is no substitute for obedient men. We must send missionaries to the lost of earth.

The believers' well-being depends on his obedience to God. Every Christian must be willing to go

in conformity to Christ's command. The Bible knows
nothing of any partial commitment which pleases
God. "To obey is better than sacrifice" said the old
prophet. The ancient sacrifice was an offering. But
God would accept no offering in the place of obedience. Nor will he now. No substitute will do. You
cannot bribe God with a gift. Obedience is bedrock
stuff. The whole moral universe rests upon it.

Too many Christians are slackers. Unwillingness
to mind God is often covered by a mumbo jumbo of
words. But deeds count. Bible language is plain as
to this. "Curse ye Meroz, said the angel of the Lord,
curse ye bitterly the inhabitants thereof; because
they came not to the help of the Lord, to the help
of the Lord against the mighty" (Judg. 5:23).

The world is a dark house. Satan, the strong man,
rules it. Half the world's population are slaves, held
in his deadly grasp. Only obedient Christians can
set those captives free. Jesus said, "Or else how can
one enter into a strong man's house, and spoil his
goods, except he first bind the strong man? and then
he will spoil his house. He that is not with me is
against me; and he that gathereth not with me scat-
tereth abroad" (Matt. 12:29,30).

We were on furlough in 1955. Our son, Danny,
then ten years old said, "What I can't understand,
Mom, is how all these preachers can preach about
going to the mission field and being missionaries,
but they don't go themselves." My wife repeated
Danny's words to me. I said, "I have been trying for
years to understand the same thing."

4. GOD DEMANDS OBEDIENCE

Jesus said pointedly, "He that hath my commandments, and keepeth them, he it is that loveth me" (John 14:21). Today men substitute orthodoxy for obedience. We attempt to put believing in the place of doing. But God is not mocked. Jesus once told the story of a man who had two sons. The man said to the first, "Son, go and work in my vineyard today." He replied, "I will not," but afterward changed his mind and went. Going to the second son he said the same to him, and he answered, "I will go, sir: and went not." Which of these two did the Father's will? They said, "The first" (Matt. 21:28-31).

How would you judge those sons? By their words, or by their deeds? The words of the second were right. But his deeds were wrong. He was orthodox, but he was disobedient. The first son was wrong in creed, but right in his deeds. His words were wrong. His works were right. He did his father's will and got credit for it. Today mission fields are white unto harvest. God's command is, "Son, daughter, go." Anything less than obedience is disobedience. This is a major cause for the apparent failure of world missions. Centuries of half-hearted missionary effort lie behind us. And unevangelized people today increase faster than we are reaching them with the gospel. This is a dramatic rebuke to our disobedience.

Tucker

A man named Tucker was successor to the noble missionary martyr, Bishop Hannington, who laid down his life for Christ in Africa. Tucker was an artist. He lived in London. Among the pictures which had made him famous was one called "Desolation." The picture shows a poor London girl dragging her fatherless child through the streets of that great city. Tears are blistering the girl's face. The whole scene appears blacker than a starless night. Finally, the picture hung in the Academy. Tucker's world-wide fame was secured.

But God spoke to Tucker and asked him if it would not be better to relieve some of the world's sorrow and suffering rather than simply to portray it on canvass. Tucker obeyed God. He gave himself to gospel ministry in the darkest slums of London. Then came news that Bishop Hannington had been murdered by the Africans. Someone was needed to take his place. Tucker said, "If it is darker than darkest London, I will go." And he set his face like a flint to go to Africa.

Tucker went to the very territory where Mwanga, a savage chief, burned little boys at the stake if they would not yield to his abominable lusts. But the day came when on that very spot one of the largest churches in the world was crowded with more than five thousand converts. Hundred of chapels all over the land were filled with Christians. Hannington obeyed God. It cost him his life. Jesus said, "Whosoever shall lose his life for my sake, and the gospel's, the same shall save it." Tucker obeyed God. God sent him to Africa. Will you obey God? That is the real issue.

Present Decisions

In the summer of 1960 I was preaching in a camp near Mason City, Nebraska. After one of the meetings, a young rancher and his wife spoke to me. He told me they had been saved not many months before. They owned a three thousand acre ranch. He

55

said they felt led to leave their ranch and go to Bible school, that their lives might be used of God for world evangelization.

The next night another young rancher and his wife spoke to me. They were neighbors of the first couple. The rancher spoke of his neighbor's decision. Then he said, "If he is willing to leave his ranch for Jesus Christ, I am willing to stay on mine and work to support him."

The first couple committed themselves to Christ and went to Bible school. The second couple committed themselves to Christ and stayed home. Which couple was more consecrated? We cannot say. Let us not try to play God. The Bible says, "Judge nothing before the time, until the Lord come" (I Cor. 4:5). What matters is that you commit your life fully to Christ. The Bible says, "The share of him who stays with the baggage shall be equal to the share of him who marches to battle" (I Sam. 30:24, Berkeley).

Will you offer yourself to Jesus Christ for world evangelization? Obedience means commitment to Christ. And obedience will be rewarded.

AMBASSADORS FOR CHRIST
(II Cor. 5:20)

"The love of Christ constraineth us" (II Cor. 5:14).
"Henceforth know we no man after the flesh"
(II Cor. 5:16).
"All things are of God" (II Cor. 5:18).

"Now then we are ambassadors for Christ" says
the Apostle Paul. We are ambassadors in Christ's
place. He came from the Father to mankind on an
all-important embassy. Now Christ is absent for a
time from the world. We are appointed in His place.
The verses preceding this striking text give reasons
why Christians are, in the divine purpose, ambassadors for Christ.

1. A NEW MOTIVATION

"The love of Christ constraineth us" writes Paul
(v. 14). "Constraineth" has been called "one of the
most expressive words in the New Testament." Paul
is not simply saying that the love of Christ for his
soul thrust him out in missionary work. Rather that
love irresistibly limits him to the one great task. It
holds him to this work to the exclusion of other con-
siderations. All his energies are forcibly com-
pressed into one channel. Says Vincent, "The idea
is not urging or driving, but shutting up to one line

and purpose, as in a narrow, walled road."

It is the love of Christ for us as shown in His death which above all else holds the apostle fast in this firm allegience. He reasons that, "If one died for all, then we're all dead." This is the central fact in Paul's theology and Christology. The scope of Christ's death is universal. In God's sight we were all judged worthy of death. When the blow fell on Christ, we were all executed in His person. Our death sentence fell on Him. We are dead in God's sight. But still we have our life to live.

Guided Power

What should the knowledge of such love do? What did it do for Paul? It held him steady in his purpose to preach the gospel in the regions beyond. It kept him "on the rails" of God's plan to evangelize the whole world. It prevented him from swerving into meaningless by-paths. When a mixture of gasoline and air is introduced into the cylinder of your car and ignited by a spark, an explosion occurs. If the same explosion occurred in the open, a flash of fire would be seen and nothing more. But in the cylinder of a car the explosion is confined. Its thrust moves the piston. There is nothing else it can do. The moving piston transmits power to the drive shaft and thus to the wheels. The love of Christ acts like that in human lives. Oh that its thrust may move us irresistibly along the lines of God's will and plan for us! "Ye shall be witnesses unto me . . . unto the uttermost part of the earth" (Acts 1:8).

"On with the message, on with the light,
  On to the regions still shrouded in night,

On to the nations that never have heard,
On with the life-giving, soul-saving Word!"

God so loved the world that He gave His Son for it. Christ so loved the world that He poured out His life for it. His love works in us to produce the desire to spend and be spent for God's glory and the salvation of souls. "Therefore," says Paul, "they that live should not henceforth live unto themselves, but unto Him . . ." It is not fair that we should live for selfish ends. Our lives are not our own. They have been bought by Christ's blood. To this C. T. Studd referred when he said, "If Jesus Christ be God, and died for me, then no sacrifice is too great for me to make for Him."

"By Love Compelled"

Studd was one of the greatest cricket players England ever produced. He was the idol of the sporting world and member of a wealthy family. But Studd became a Christian. He turned his back on the bright glitter of fame and went to China as a missionary. When his twenty-fifth birthday came he inherited a large sum of money. He decided to give his money to spread the gospel and trust God to supply his own needs. He sent D. L. Moody $20,000 to start the Moody Bible Institute. Other sums were sent elsewhere for God's work until not a cent remained.

His friends asked, "Why did you give all your money away? You are a poor man now."

Studd laughed, "Poor? How can I be poor? My Heavenly Father owns the whole world. I can write checks on the bank of heaven!"

After some years Studd was forced to leave China because of asthma. His health gradually improved in England. He went to India. There he worked for years until asthma again forced him back to England. Doctors warned that further missionary work would mean death.

Faith's Laugh

One day he saw a sign outside an English church. It read, "Cannibals need missionaries." Studd laughed and laughed when he saw it. Soon he was bound for Africa. Far inland this English gentleman built a hut among the natives. The roof was grass, the floor, dried mud. In one corner was a native bed. In the middle stood a rough homemade table and chair. Studd called his new home, "Buckingham Palace." To help reach millions he himself could not reach he founded the World-wide Evangelization Crusade. He spent the rest of his life in Africa in active service for Christ until he died in 1931. He was never sorry for the career he gave up.

"How could you make such a sacrifice?" he was once asked. Studd's answer has already been given. "Sacrifice? If Jesus Christ be God, and died for me, then no sacrifice is too great for me to make for Him." Twenty-two words! But a whole life is required to live them out in practical obedience.

2. A NEW ORIENTATION

What does Paul mean by stating, "Henceforth know we no man after the flesh?" (v. 16). He has told us One died for all. Therefore, Christ is universal Redeemer. The same One rose again. Therefore Christ is universal Lord. His boundless sacrifice was made for all. His infinite claim is the same upon all men everywhere. No race or class or social caste can boast of special prerogatives with Him. At the cross all carnal distinctions die.

Another version says, "From now on we think of no one in terms of his purely human nature." Our present relation to Christ is utterly different from that based on ordinary human standards. Even kinship to Jesus "after the flesh" would be no basis of Christian privilege. To have eaten and drunk in His presence, to have listened to His voice on earth, would confer no special distinction in God's kingdom. Christ has not done more for His brothers and for those who companied with Him on earth than He has done for all mankind. Among Christians carnal distinctions disappear.

Before and After

It is evident Paul had some knowledge of Christ before His conversion. That knowledge was received through normal human channels. It was limited to reports of Christ's appearance, His activities, His contacts with the Jews and His trial and crucifixion. But when the risen and glorified Christ spoke directly to him out of heaven, Paul asked, "Who art thou?"

Paul's meaning is clear. To know a man "after the flesh" is to know him by outward evidences. What are the circumstances of his life? What of his wealth, station, culture, knowledge? But Paul no longer judges men by those standards. With him the one question is whether a man has claimed the place which the death of Christ has secured him. Is he living in Christ as a new creature? "If any one is in Christ, he is a new creation." That is Paul's point of view. From the perspective he considers every man. "So if you have been raised to life in fellowship with Christ, keep on seeking the things above, where Christ is seated at the right hand of God."

A New Creation

What has changed the whole basis of Paul's judgment? It is the resurrection of Jesus Christ. After that event Christ must no longer be thought of in mere human terms. He is now recognized as spiritual Lord of God's new creation. All relations are different this side of the resurrection. Revelation presents Him to us as the very Son of God. This certainty reduces mere human knowledge of Him to a secondary and inferior plane.

Therefore, every man who has enthroned Christ in life has entered a new realm of being. His outlook on life has changed totally. To him everything is different. The selfish carnal views of himself, of his fellowmen, and of Christ have passed away. Like snow in the springtime melts before the ever brighter rays of the advancing sun, so the "things" of the old life pass away in the warmth and light of new resurrection life in Christ.

3. A NEW MAGNIFICATION OF GOD

"All things are of God" (v. 18). Let us mark well who performs these wonders. It is God alone who opens this new realm to those who turn to Him in repentance and faith. God alone has dealt with the sin of the world. We must not fail to discern His primary agency in this moral transformation. All things involved in this mighty miracle of change are from God. He is the sole author and mover of the wonderful facts Paul has been describing. Man can claim no credit for these things. This is as true of the most committed, dedicated men as it is of those who deny all that God has done for them. God did the work, and God gave us this ministry which we must discharge to every creature.

Happy indeed is the Christian who magnifies God as he participates in world evangelization. Before me lies a letter from an Iowa farmer who, with his family, has supported a missionary couple in Africa for twenty years. Farming, for that family, has meant reaching lost souls in Africa. Not only Mother and Dad, but all the children have been vitally interested.

The Letter (in part)

"Our daughter has felt the call to the mission fields. She has graduated from college and is now in her third year of nurses' training. We trust the Lord will find an open door for her. We love to have our children with us, but we feel a burden for lost souls and want His will to be done.

"Times are getting a little more difficult on the farm. The support of missionaries went up by $200 last year while the price of corn goes down each year. But we have an almighty God and trust that He will continue to use us in His work. Please pray for us. We are reluctant concerning our testimony in your writing. If there is any glory involved, we want our Lord to have it. But if you think it will help the cause of missions, you may go ahead with it."

Should not such a letter encourage us? Surely it must. Let us write one sentence on our hearts. "If there is any glory involved, we want our Lord to have it." That was the desire of Paul's heart. "All things are of God." Let us labor for world evangelization as though everything depended upon us. But let us be quick to give glory to Him who alone makes possible our life and labor. "To God be the glory, great things He hath done."

Borne along by the dynamic force of the truth he is uttering Paul declares, "We are ambassadors for Christ." The only other place the expression is used is in Ephesians 6:20. There Paul says, "I am an ambassador in bonds." Our bonds and fetters are less brutal than those the great apostle knew. But we are nonetheless hampered and restricted in our efforts toward a wider outreach to men still unreached. Shall we settle back in easy resignation? God forbid! The love of Christ constrains us. We know Him. We live on the "new creation" side of the resurrection. All is of God. We take courage and go forward with Him.

WHY PREACH IN REGIONS BEYOND?

"Having hope . . . to preach the gospel in the regions beyond you" (II Cor. 10:15,16).

The Apostle Paul was never content to keep the gospel within the Christian community. In the gospel Paul had something the world needed and he knew it. He expressed his desire to the Corinthian Christians in this way. "Having hope," he wrote, "to preach the gospel in the regions beyond you." Why did Paul say that? Why did Paul strive to carry the gospel to regions beyond? Why did he want to get God's message past the Christian frontier? This is the question I would like to consider with you. For it has to do with us. There are still regions beyond, areas where Christ is little known or unknown. Why should we preach the gospel there?

1. CHRIST'S MISSIONARY COMMAND INCLUDES THE REGIONS BEYOND

This missionary command was given several times by the risen Lord. Just what did He command His followers to do before He should return? The Bible answers this question in final chapters of the Gospels and the first chapter of Acts. Five chapters of the New Testament contain the plainest information in the world about Christ's missionary command. In Matthew He says, "Disciple all nations." In Mark He says, "Go ye into all the world, and preach the gospel to every creature." In Luke He says, "That repentance and remission of sins should be preached in his name among all nations." In John He says, "As my Father hath sent me, even so send I you." In Acts He says, "Ye shall be witnesses unto me . . . unto the uttermost part of the earth." Yes, Christ commanded His Church to carry the gospel to the whole world. This includes the regions beyond. These are our orders.

Years ago there was a bad train wreck in the east. Two trains came together head-on. As one of the dying engineers was lifted from the smashed cab of his overturned engine, his fumbling fingers drew a yellow paper from an inner pocket of his work jacket. "Take this," he said weakly, "it will show you I was given wrong orders." The engineer insisted he was not to blame for the tragic wreck. His orders were wrong. But no Christian at the judgment will be able to defend his missionary failure with such an argument. The Bible will shut his mouth. Christ said, "Go, make disciples among all nations. Preach the gospel to every creature. Be witnesses unto me unto the uttermost part of the earth." Our orders are clear. They include the regions beyond.

2. OUR LORD'S ILLUSTRATIONS INCLUDE THE REGIONS BEYOND

He said, "The field is the world." Our Lord here compares the missionary task to the work of a farmer. The farmer prepares the soil, sows the seed, fights the weeds, and finally reaps the harvest. Remember, the field is the world. Have we sown the gospel seed everywhere in the world? Have we shared the good news equally in all lands? No, we have not. We have been selfish. We have repeatedly sown the gospel seed in a few favored parts of the world. We have desired its benefits for ourselves and for our children. We have almost forgotten the people in far-off lands. In this we have done wrong. We have not obeyed our Master's command.

In Argentina I had a plot of some five acres of ground. An Argentine, Manuel Burgeno, asked if he could cultivate the land. I told him to go ahead. Burgeno did a good job on the part of the field he cultivated. But he left more than an acre untouched by the plow. I asked him why he left that ground uncultivated. He said, "Too hard." Is that our attitude toward world evangelization? We favor the easy places. Are the unreached places too hard?

Starved

I remind you of a second metaphor Christ used. He said, "I am the bread of life." Christ declares that He is essential food. Without Him no man can live. He said again, "For the bread of God is he which comes down from heaven and gives life to the world." We Americans do not understand the meaning of physical hunger. Millions of people in other lands suffer hunger pangs by day and by night. They never have enough to eat.

Ray Davis, associate director of the Sudan Interior Mission, has spent many years in Nigeria, West Africa. He told us of a time when three years of drought had afflicted a great section of that land. He said, "As we sat down to eat our modest meal, we could see groups of famished, emaciated people outside our home. Hungry little children were crying for food their starving parents were unable to give them." Said Davis, "Often it was simply impossible for us to eat our own food."

Oh that we might feel compassion for multitudes that starve spiritually. They lack the gospel we have failed to give them. Christ is the bread of life without which no man can live. Men unreached by the gospel are dead. Unless the gospel reaches them they must remain forever dead. Jesus said, "Except ye eat the flesh of the Son of Man . . . ye have no life in you." Remember, we need not murder Africans or Asians or Latin Americans with machine guns or atom bombs to be guilty of their blood. We need only withhold the gospel from them.

Light a Lamp

Another metaphor our Lord used was that of light. He said, "I am the light of the world." Wicked men thought they had put out that light when Jesus was crucified. But the light had passed to other lives. Jesus had said to His followers, "Ye are the light of the world." If the light we have is for the world, dare we keep it from part of the world? It is good to have large beautiful lights in your living room and dining room. But if you leave the back entrance in utter darkness, someone may fall down the cellar steps. So with gospel light. Men out yonder grope in the blackness and shadow of death. Every soul in the darkness of heathendom is waiting on us. We must send the light. We must light a gospel lamp within sight of every man on earth.

Just One Way

Still another of Jesus' metaphors was that of the way. He said, "I am the way . . . no man cometh unto the Father but by me." There is one way that leads men to God. Just one. Think of those who do not know the way. Missionary Duane Stous told me in Paraguay of the night he found the way to life while others died. Stous was in California with other Christian fellows training for missionary service. They were called out to fight forest fires. Divided into five man squads they battled the flames all day. Darkness had fallen when someone brought sandwiches. They stood eating ravenously. Suddenly a call came from the ridge road above them. "The fire has broken through! Run for your lives!"

Stous and a companion started upward toward the road. The other men ran down the canyon. Desperately the two men climbed. The billowing heat, the hellish flames came closer. It was awful. Death was at their backs. More than once strength seemed gone. Finally they staggered on to the road. A car came. They circled around to the mouth of the canyon where they hoped to meet the other fellows. Through the long night they searched. They called and called. In vain they listened. No reply. Daylight brought the awful answer. Fourteen charred bodies lay on the canyon floor. Fiery death had overtaken the fleeing men. Jesus Christ is the only way for men to reach heaven. His solemn meaning is clear beyond question. "No man," He said, "cometh unto the Father but by me."

3. CHRIST'S ILLUSTRATIONS AND COMMANDS SHOW THAT TO PREACH THE GOSPEL IN THE REGIONS BEYOND IS BASIC TO GOD'S PLAN

Let us imagine ourselves standing on a distant star, looking back at our globe. God had a lost world on His hands. The Bible says that "By one man sin entered into the world, and death by sin; and so death passed upon all men, for that all have sinned" (Rom. 5:12). Again we read concerning mankind, "For all have sinned, and come short of the glory of God." The Bible removes any doubt we may have about men being lost. It is not a question of how many sins a person must commit in order to be lost.

Lost Already

The truth is that Jesus Christ came into the world to face the horror of Calvary because men were lost already. The Bible says, "He that believeth not [on Christ] is condemned already, because he hath not believed" (John 3:18). Christ himself puts this fact beyond all argument. He says He came into the world "to seek and to save that which was lost." God provided one way to save lost men. He was willing to send His Son. And God's Son was willing to come as the "Lamb slain from the foundation of the world." For this we praise God.

But is praise our whole business? No. It is not enough. We must obey God. We must reach the unreached with the gospel. If not, we leave them to die never knowing. They cannot know of Christ unless we tell them. Unless they know, they cannot live. We must tell them. This is man's part of redemption's plan. God's part is the death and resurrection of Christ. Man's part is the preaching of repentance and forgiveness of sins in Christ's name among all nations.

4. THE CONDEMNED MILLIONS IN REGIONS BEYOND HAVE HIGHEST PRIORITY FOR GOSPEL PREACHING

It is not just that the unreached millions are lost. That alone is worse than we can understand. It is not simply that those millions, as the Bible says, remain "dead in trespasses and sins." It is not alone the fact that they are "without hope and without God." These facts are true of unsaved people everywhere. They apply to men and women of privileged intellect among the most enlightened nations. To remain unsaved anywhere is dreadful.

But the unreached of earth cannot help themselves without our help. This fact should underlie all our Christian activity. The Word of God is very plain. It says, "Whosoever shall call upon the name of the Lord shall be saved" (Rom. 10:13). If that statement were not qualified we might take it to mean that any pagan without gospel light could cry to God and be saved. But the Bible qualifies that statement. It goes on, "How then shall they call on him in whom they have not believed? and how shall they believe in him of whom they have not heard? and how shall they hear without a preacher? And how shall they preach, except they be sent?" There, bold and plain, the task of the Church is set forth: bear the gospel to all men.

Which unsaved man most deserves your help? The one who can hear the gospel or the one who cannot? What group most needs your help? Those who can hear the gospel, or those who cannot? To ask the question is to answer it. Hundreds of tribes still wait for the first portion of God's Word to be translated into their language. Who are the young people willing to make those translations? Who are the men and women who will pray them out to the field? Who will work to support them? Who, Christian, if not you? Great metropolitan areas in many lands are unevangelized. Who will go to do that job? Who will support those who go? Who will give them power through prayer? Who, Christian, if not you?

World evangelization means to offer Christ to all men everywhere. We cannot justify the neglect of unreached areas. To be sure there are many worthy causes. But no other causes occupies first place with God. This one does. God has spoken on this matter. He commands us to finish this work. It is wrong for us to pour large efforts into other things simply because they are good. The good may be the enemy of the best. If Christians would give all to get the gospel to the regions beyond, the world task could soon be finished.

Good, or Best

Weigh carefully the difference between doing things which are good and doing that which is best. The difference is illustrated by the tragic experience of a drawbridge operator. This man, years ago, operated the drawbridge at Passaic, New Jersey. One afternoon he had opened the bridge to let a boat pass. His boy was playing nearby. Suddenly from a distance sounded the whistle of an oncoming express train. The operator realized in a flash he had blundered. The bridge should have been closed. Instantly he threw the levers. At that moment he was horrified to see his boy slip and fall into the river.

The father faced a hard choice. His boy was drowning. Every instinct urged him to leap to the rescue. But another duty came first. Hundreds of passengers' lives were at stake. The man knew it. He stayed at his post. The bridge slammed into position. Seconds later the train thundered safely across. Only then did the father leap to save his boy. But he was too late. Life had gone when the body was recovered. Did that father do right? Yes, he did. He faced a difficult choice. To have saved his boy would have been good. But to save the passengers was his first responsibility. That father, under awful pressure, chose what was best.

Christian, your choice may not be so difficult as that. But it is similar. Do good wherever you can. But make the main thrust of your life that of taking Christ to earth's unreached masses. Many kinds of help are needed. Keep your vision clear. Make your commitment to Christ real. God will show you what to do.

THE CHURCH'S CRIME

> "If thou forbear to deliver them that are drawn
> unto death, and those that are ready to be slain;
> If thou sayest, Behold, we knew it not; doth not
> he that pondereth the heart consider it? and he
> that keepeth thy soul, doth not he know it? and
> shall not he render to every man according to his
> works?" (Prov. 24:11,12).

I remember a long ago school day in Lincoln, Nebraska. It was September 17, 1930. About midmorning I heard the sound of a siren. Was it a fire engine or a police car? I wondered. It was neither. At 10:00 a.m. that morning a dark blue buick sedan pulled up next to the Lincoln National Bank and Trust Company at the northwest corner of 12th & O. As the bank opened its doors, six men left the car. Four entered the bank. They looked like businessmen but they were not. In less than ten minutes gangsters had pulled off, without much trouble, the largest bank robbery in United States history. Their loot was more than $2,700,000. What a tremendous loss! It broke the bank. But our text talks of another kind of loss. It is not of dollars but of souls. This loss defies comparison.

1. THE GHASTLY REALITY

It is presented in these words, "Them that are drawn unto death, and those that are ready to be slain." Who are these people? Our text does not name them. But the Bible describes a vast multitude to whom these words fitly apply. They are the un-evangelized people of earth. Unevangelized means that they have never heard the gospel. They could not be saved if they would. They have no knowledge of the way of salvation. As the Apostle Paul says, "How then shall they call on him in whom they have not believed? and how shall they believe in him of whom they have not heard?" (Rom. 10:14).

Where do these doomed souls live? Many are in South America. The heart of that continent is one of the last gospel frontiers. Hundreds of tribes of unreached people have been discovered in New Guinea. The unevangelized are humanity's neglected masses. Their total probably reaches the staggering figure of one billion four hundred million human beings. No one can visualize such a quantity of people.

What will be the fate of people who have never heard the gospel? Opinions are worth nothing here. Only revelation can answer this inquiry. Has God plainly told us in the Bible the fate of men un-reached with the gospel? He has. Must unevangel-ized souls be lost? The Bible says they are lost even now. All men out of Christ are lost. "He that believ-eth on him is not condemned: but he that believeth not is condemned already, because he hath not be-lieved in the name of the only begotten Son of God" (John 3:18).

Sobering Truth

"Surely," someone argues, "John 3:18 does not mean that." Compare this text with others. Paul wrote, "Wherefore, as by one man sin entered into the world, and death by sin; and so death passed upon all men, for that all have sinned" (Rom. 5:12). Death passed upon all men. Death is in the saddle and means to ride every sinner into hell. Can any man escape? Christ's answer is clear. "I am the way, the truth, and the life" (John 14:6). What Christian does not know that text? But notice the last part of it. Jesus says, "No man cometh unto the Father, but by me." No man will reach heaven without Christ. To this agreed Peter's word at Pentecost. "Neither is there salvation in any other: for there is none other name under heaven given among men, whereby we must be saved" (Acts 4:12).

Thus text after text marches forward and gives its testimony. The evidence is conclusive. Sad, unutterably sad, is the condition of men who have never heard of Christ. They live in night. They die in darkness. Their eternity is the blackness of darkness forever. Christian, those warning texts should ring like alarm gongs in the bell tower of your heart.

Doing Nothing

"But what is our crime?" someone asks. "Is it our fault that people die unreached?" To this the Bible answers, "If thou forbear to deliver . . ." That simply means, "If you do nothing." To damn these people, Christians have but to leave them alone. By doing nothing we doom them forever. There is no need to drive a dagger into their hearts, or choke them to death one by one. To destroy them we need only let them die, as they now live, knowing not the gospel.

Christians must face this responsibility. The letter I received from Andres Robert, a dear Argentine friend, states, "We are praying that you may receive a new filling and vision of the Holy Spirit for this poor continent of South America. Like a great ship it is sinking more deeply every day in the mire of sin. Soon the ship will be totally submerged. Every opportunity will have passed, and every hope of salvation will have gone."

2. THE GLIB REPLY

"We knew it not." This is a plausible excuse. Christians are apt to say this at the judgment. Charged with the death of souls they will defend themselves with a plea of ignorance. They will deny that they knew the condition of the heathen. This is the pathetic case of multitudes of Christians. They do not know the Bible basis of world evangelization. They know as little about missions as a baby does about mathematics. But why this ignorance? The Bible has been neglected!

The Word of God will condemn us if we pay it no heed. October 24, 1960, I boarded a Boeing 707 plane in Chicago. The man to my left, I noticed, was reading a Sunday school paper. I felt he might be a Christian desiring to witness. "You seem very interested in that Sunday school paper," I suggested.

"Yes," he said, "this is the sort of my vocation, teaching Sunday school."

I replied, "So teaching Sunday school is your vocation. What would you say is the Christian's true vocation or mission in life?"

He hesitated a few moments, then said, "I think we should glorify God."

I said, "Right. But there is something more definite? What is God trying to do in our age? Does God have a purpose in the world?" The man could not answer. He remained perplexed. I hinted that the answer was to be found in each of the Gospels and in the first chapter of Acts. But the man was baffled. How sad for a Sunday school teacher not to know God's plan to evangelize the world.

A Poor Excuse

Many Christians are like that. Yet ignorance is no excuse. The Bible often repeats Christ's command, "Go ye into the world, and preach the gospel to every creature." Dare we say, "We knew it not"?

We know that 94 out of every 100 preachers in the world minister to less than 10 per cent of the world's people. This in spite of Christ's statement, "The field is the world." This despite our Lord's plea for His other sheep which must be brought to the fold. How can we say, "We knew it not"?

We know that half the world still waits to hear the gospel. Upon these unevangelized souls the dark forces of hell advance with incredible speed. Communism today rules the destinies of almost a billion people. We cannot say we did not know.

We cannot say we thought missions was a secondary matter. Christ said, "I am the bread of life." He also said, "Except ye eat the flesh of the Son of man, and drink his blood, ye have no life in you" (John 6:53). It would be folly for us to insist, "We knew it not."

There is deadly danger in this glib reply. Let us resist the common temptation to fool ourselves. It is so easy for us to believe what we wish to believe. I recall when I spoke to a men's group in New Orleans. The message dealt with Christ's command, and the awful need of unreached men. Afterward the chairman led in prayer. He prayed, "Oh God, thou knowest that there are parts of New Orleans that are just as dark as darkest Africa." I felt like interrupting him. Why? Because that statement is false. New Orleans has been evangelized. Africa has not. In New Orleans any seeking soul can find a church. In New Orleans anyone can hear the gospel by radio. In New Orleans anyone can get a Bible. In New Orleans anyone can obtain Christian literature. In vast areas of Africa these things are not true.

3. THE GRIM RECKONING

"Doth not he that pondereth the heart consider it? and he that keepeth thy soul, doth not he know it? and shall not he render to every man according to his works?" These words tell of a coming judgment. Any Christian can be selfish now. Mark it well. God does nothing in haste. He does not rush to judgment. God lets every man show fully what is in his heart. But the eyes of God are constantly upon the motives of men. God sees, God knows. The day is coming when accounts must be rendered. The Apostle Paul says, "We must all appear before the judgment seat of Christ" (II Cor. 5:10). No excuse will stand the test of that hour. There will be no dodging. Sins of omission will be judged. Christians who refused the gospel to lost men will be faced with their crime.

What a solemn hour that will be. People ask whether a man can be saved who has never heard the gospel. It might be better to ask whether a man can be saved who has never given the gospel to the heathen. Not that salvation is by works. But what of a man who knows others are dying without Christ, yet shuts his heart against them? Can a man belong to Christ and have none of Christ's compassion? The Bible says, "If any man have not the Spirit of Christ, he is none of his" (Rom. 8:9). Can the Holy Spirit be in a man's life without manifesting His presence?

Willing to Go

God will deal with Christians who could have gone, but did not. There are thousands like that. Many Christians have told me with deep regret of their failure to enter missionary service. From every congregation missionaries should go. I am sometimes charged with preaching that every Christian should go as a missionary. That is not true. But every Christian should commit himself wholly to Christ. World evangelization is the vocation of every Christian. God has made it so. Every Christian should be willing to go. Each should honestly seek and obey the will of God for his life.

In the spring of 1955 I flew from Costa Rica to the United States. A businessman boarded the plane at Honduras. We began to talk. The man was a lumberman. For years he operated a mill in Louisiana. As timber got scarce he moved his mill. Finally business got very poor. The man heard there was lumber in Honduras. He made provision for his wife and children in Louisiana, then went to Honduras. There he built a mill. When I met him he had been traveling back and forth for several years. His family was in Louisiana. His work was in Honduras. "What a life of sacrifice!" I thought. But the man was cheerful. He was willing to face hardships. Why? To make money! Christian, the world puts us to shame. Men are willing to do for gold what we are unwilling to do for God.

Blood Guilt

Some will answer at the judgment for the blood of lost men. Hear this word from the Old Testament, "When I say unto the wicked, Thou shalt surely die; and thou givest him not warning . . . the same wicked man shall die in his iniquity; but his blood will I require at thine hand" (Ezek. 3:18). Here is a sinning African. He is never reached by the gospel. He will die in his sin. But the Christian who could have gotten the gospel to him and failed, will answer for the African's blood. That is what God says. This principle is in force in our age. Hear Paul's words to the Ephesians: "I am pure from the blood of all men" (Acts 20:26). Paul declares with what faithfulness, tears and suffering he had given the whole counsel of God in Ephesus. If Paul had not shared God's truth with those men he would have been guilty of their blood. This is true of us.

Pardon Concealed

In the Isle of Man years ago there perished one of the best governors the Isle ever had. In time of war he was accused of treason and sentenced to be hanged. Afterward it was found that he had been falsely judged and a pardon was issued. But the pardon fell into the hands of a bitter enemy who kept it locked up until after the governor had been executed. The Word of God says that all men without Christ are already condemned. Men do not have to do anything to be lost. They are lost already. Their only hope of salvation is in Jesus Christ.

Paul says, "Whosoever shall call upon the name of the Lord shall be saved" (Rom. 10:13). The great apostle then binds every Christian with a chain of logic: "How then shall they call on him in whom they have not believed? and how shall they believe in him of whom they have not heard? and how shall they hear without a preacher? And how shall they preach, except they be sent?" Christian, one day you received a pardon signed in the blood of the Son of God. That pardon offers life to every condemned man. All men are under sentence of death. What have you done? Are you locking up the pardon?

Unless you and I are doing all we can to get the gospel to unreached men, we are sinning against men and against God. This is the Church's crime. Let us have no more excuses. Christ's command to evangelize the world still stands. Give yourself in obedient submission to Him, and do your part in that task.

MISSIONARY PURPOSE

"I have appeared unto thee for this purpose, to
make thee a minister and a witness both of these
things which thou hast seen, and of those things
in the which I will appear unto thee" (Acts 26:16).

The Bible tells of a man who hated Christians.
He breathed out "threat and murder" against the
Lord's disciples. But God knocked him down. And
this man, Paul, became the greatest missionary since
the time of Christ. God said to Paul in the very act
of transforming his life, "I have appeared unto thee
for this purpose." God revealed to Paul His purpose.
God's purpose was to make Christ known to all mankind. God has a purpose. It affects you. Will you
think about it?

1. PURPOSE

In all human life, purpose is enormously important. It is a vital ingredient of success. It is essential to all real achievement. Purpose precedes success. Show me a man who is making a mark on the
world, and I will show you a man dominated by
some purpose. The man's purpose may be good, or
it may be bad. But every man who is outstanding
today, somewhere back along the line got an idea.

That idea, that vision, was transformed into a purpose and has made the man what he is today.

Take the case of the Prophet Daniel. Early in life, "Daniel purposed in his heart" (Dan. 1:8). The young captive lad had a high aim. The life that follows is perhaps without parallel in history. Daniel mounted from one position to another by the sheer ascendance of his moral greatness. He started as a slave boy in a powerful pagan society. In that society of indulgent, selfish, time-serving men, Daniel gradually stood out from all the rest. He could be trusted. Daniel could not be bought. Thus he rose higher and higher like a shining star. His long and useful life spanned the reign of three kings, honored God, and has inspired the hearts of countless thousands from that remote time to the present day. "Daniel purposed in his heart."

Aimlessness is a curse. The man who aims at nothing generally hits it. Education without purpose leaves a man like a ship without a helmsman or a car without a driver. Years ago I picked up a hitchhiker, a graduate of the University of Wisconsin. He was a pleasant chap. He seemed well equipped mentally. But he confessed he had no goal. Life for him had no destination. He told me he hoped to go to Europe and enlist in some army. Why? Simply because he knew nothing better to do. Such a case spells tragedy.

Purpose makes a man outstanding. It is a living thing. Years ago at Moody Bible Institute in Chicago I heard a man speak. His name was T. J. Bach. He said that when he was a student in the institute they called him, "The little man with a screw loose in his head and nuts about South America." But

Bach had a noble aim. It energized his whole life. He went to South America. There he wrote his name imperishably in the annals of missionary endeavor. His long, fruitful life has been a blessing to countless thousands across the world.

2. HIGHEST PURPOSE

Every person should seek life's highest purpose. Can it be found? Yes, it can. What is life's highest purpose? The Christian calls it "the will of God." The noblest purpose any life can fulfill is the thing God had in mind when He called that life into being. Paul said, "Be ye not unwise, but understanding what the will of the Lord is" (Eph. 5:17). Would God mock us? Would He command us to do His will and give us no way to know it? Surely not. Unless a person can know God's will for his life, existence is just a gamble. Rule God out, and what is life? Nothing but a bucket of ashes. Anything less than knowing God's will means a sadly empty life.

Grenfell of Labrador, the famous Christian doctor, often spoke of the night he was saved. Grenfell would say, "I was converted from a life of drifting to a life of direction. I found my compass that night." Grenfell's later work proved he had "found his compass."

Then the burning question comes, "How can a person know God's plan for his life? How does God reveal His will?" You will find God's will in the Bible, or nowhere! God has spoken to mankind through the Bible as in no other way. Someone may say, "God speaks to me in nature." Or, "God speaks to me through a beautiful sunset." What does he mean? He senses the presence of God in growing things, or he thrills to something divine in the glory of the setting sun. But neither the beauty of nature nor the crimson western sky can transmit to anyone the knowledge of God's will for his life.

Revealed

In the Bible, God speaks. How majestically the Book of Hebrews begins, "God, who at sundry times and in divers manners spake in time past unto the fathers by the prophets, Hath in these last days spoken unto us by his Son." The Lord Jesus is the living Word of God. He came to earth, died, rose again, and went back to heaven. Since then God's written Word has been completed and given to mankind in hundreds of different languages. This is man's chief treasure, the Holy Bible. Our Lord said, "Search the scriptures" (John 5:39). Paul said, "All scripture is given by inspiration of God, and is profitable" (II Tim. 3:16). Elsewhere Paul advised, "Give attendance to reading" (I Tim. 4:13) or, in modern English, "Read the Bible." Life's highest purpose is revealed in the Bible.

I well remember when I determined to read the Bible to find out whether God had a plan. I was a Christian. I knew the Bible was the Word of God. I loved the Book. At that time I resolved to read the New Testament straight through with one idea: to seek God's purpose. Did I find it? I did! From the Gospels to the Revelation the New Testament marks out God's plan. Christians must go and preach the gospel to every human being. To evangelize the world is God's goal for our age. There is no question about this. God's Word is plain. The Bible says there will be people in heaven, redeemed by the blood of

Christ, from every kindred, tongue, people, and nation. In Isaiah's words, "This is the purpose that is purposed upon the whole earth."

A Clear Goal

Our God-given task must be finished. Christ said, "You shall be witnesses unto me . . . to the uttermost part of the earth." Dare we stop short? No. The whole job must be done. During nineteen hundred years, part of the task has been accomplished. Our own land is more thoroughly evangelized today than any land on earth. A question arises. To what people are Christians most responsible? The Bible answers: To those not yet reached by the gospel. God's goal in this age is not a converted world. Rather, it is a world evangelized. We must go to distant lands. We must offer Christ to every man. The church should never dig in behind a fixed battle line. But our world goal has been long obscured. The church has settled into a sort of trench warfare. Let us lift the battle shout: "Over the top to reach the unreached."

3. PURPOSE SUCCEEDS

Your life in God's hands will accomplish the purpose God planned for you. The Prophet Jeremiah said, "Every purpose of the Lord shall be performed" (Jer. 51:29). So give yourself to Him. Give your whole self! Make a decisive commitment to God. Mind you, God's purpose for your life has a solid Bible basis. This is no fanciful dream. You are asked to do nothing on the basis of mere emotion. King Solomon said, "Every purpose is established by counsel" (Prov. 20:18). Go for counsel to the New Testament. Go again and again. The Lord Jesus said, "Heaven and earth shall pass away: but my words shall not pass away" (Mark 13:31). Read and reread those Bible verses that explain God's plan. Meditate much on our Lord's words concerning world evangelization. Check your bearings. Verify your conclusions. Then press straight for the goal.

Move With God

Like a mighty current freighted with eternal consequences, God's purpose to evangelize the world sweeps through the New Testament. It connects in the past with God's former revelations. Our Lord declares that His death, resurrection, and plan to evangelize the world fulfill Old Testament Scriptures. This fact gives enormous significance to the missionary enterprise. When Columbus and his men sailed into the mouth of the Orinoco River, whose tremendous impulse carries fresh water far out to sea, someone suggested that they had discovered an island. "No," said Columbus, "this is no island. This mighty current drains the waters of a continent." That was true. And so it is with world evangelization. The current of this mighty movement carries in its bosom, from the upper headwaters of God's earlier dealings with mankind, His plan from eternity to eternity.

God longs for you to make His purpose your purpose. In love He commands you to participate in the work of missions. In this way your life will count for eternal values. Paul said of the Macedonians that they, "first gave their own selves to the Lord, and unto us by the will of God" (II Cor. 8:5). Do that. Give yourself wholly to the Lord in glad surrender. Then seek a way to serve in some phase of God's global enterprise.

Finish the Job

Shall we not finish the work God has given us to do? Almost two thousand years have passed since Christ commanded that the world be evangelized. Part of the task has been done. Shall we not press on to the finish. Oh to reach the unreached! Oh to preach Christ to those who have never heard His blessed name! Let that be the high aim of every Christian's life.

Our Lord lived that way. He came to earth to die. He set His face like a flint to go to Jerusalem. He said, "My meat is to do the will of him who sent me, and to finish his work." Again he said, "I must work the works of him that sent me while it is yet day." As His life on earth drew to an end He could pray to His Father saying, "I have finished the work which thou gavest me to do." At last on the cross He bore God's wrath against sin. All was accomplished to make possible our redemption. Then He said, "It is finished" (John 19:30). Christian, identify yourself with God's purpose for world evangelization. Then stick to the job. Stay on course. Go for the goal.

Paul's Aim

The Apostle Paul did that. God stopped Paul on the Damascus Road and flooded his soul with light. From then on Paul understood that the will of God was world evangelization. Let us call Paul to the witness stand.

"Paul," we ask, "will you be true? Will you mind God about missions?"

Paul's answer rings down across the years, "I was not disobedient unto the heavenly vision" (Acts 26:19).

"But Paul," says a friend, "don't go to Europe. There is plenty of need for gospel preaching right here at Jerusalem."

Paul pulls free, saying, "I am debtor both to the Greeks, and to the Barbarians; both to the wise, and to the unwise" (Rom. 1:14).

"Paul, don't be a fanatic. There are a lot of people in Judea who are unsaved."

Paul answers, "So have I strived to preach the gospel, not where Christ was named, lest I should build upon another man's foundation: But as it is written, To whom he was not spoken of, they shall see: and they that have not heard shall understand" (Rom. 15:20,21).

"Now Paul, be reasonable. You are going to get killed in this missionary business if you aren't more careful."

Paul only says, "None of these things move me, neither count I my life dear unto myself, so that I might finish my course with joy, and the ministry, which I have received of the Lord Jesus, to testify the gospel of the grace of God" (Acts 20:24).

This Life Wins

On and on Paul goes. Threats can't thwart his purpose. Criticism can't crush him. Stonings can't stop him. Nor can jails, nor perils, nor persecutions, nor punishments, nor anything that men or devils could hurl at him. Though the way was long and lonely, Paul passionately persevered until at last he could say, "For I am now ready to be offered, and the time of my departure is at hand. I have fought a good fight, I have finished my course, I have kept the faith" (II Tim. 4:6,7).

Paul had a purpose. He had a good purpose. Best of all, he had God's purpose. He found what God wanted done and gave himself to Christ for that job with glorious abandon. Paul never stopped working for world evangelization until they cut his head off. That was his promotion to the visible presence of his King.

"God is no respecter of persons." He offers to you the same essential opportunity He offered Paul. God's command is plain. He wants your life. Whether praying, giving, going, or helping in some other way, missions is your job. Don't dodge it. Don't delay. Face it. Fight it out with yourself if necessary. But settle it. Yield to God. Say to Him, "Here I am, Lord. I take my hands off my life. Lead me. Show me your place for me in world evangelization." This is the way. Will you take it?

WORLD EVANGELIZATION
BROUGHT NEAR

"All authority hath been given unto me in heaven and on earth. Go ye therefore, and make disciples of all the nations, baptizing them in the name of the Father and of the Son and of the Holy Spirit: teaching them to observe all things whatsoever I commanded you: and lo, I am with you always, even unto the end of the world" (Matt. 28:18-20, ASV).

The verses of our text are very practical. They tell us what God is doing in our times. God has shared what is on His heart with you and me. Is this not wonderful? Consider

1. GOD'S GREAT PLAN

The evangelization of the world is God's present purpose. Jesus Christ is sending saved men among the nations to win others to Him. Individual converts are won. This is done by spiritual power. Jesus said, "No man can come unto me except my Father draw him." No sword or gun compels conversion. World-wide the gospel goes. God commands that His pardon be offered to all. Every person must be reached. What an undertaking! There has been nothing like it in the world's history.

Its Span

God's plan is great in its span. It arches across history like a high suspension bridge. Where is the bridge anchored? Did world evangelization spring from teachings of Christ? He tells us the historic anchorage is farther back. "Thus it is written . . . that repentance and remission of sins should be preached in his name among all nations" (Luke 24:46, 47). "It is written" shows that God's missionary purpose was recorded in the Old Testament.

We look forward along the sweeping arch of this bridge of evangelization. We try to see its future extreme. When will the work be done? The disciples asked Christ when this age would end. His answer in part was, "The gospel must first be published among all nations" (Mark 13:10). The bridge of missions is well supported. At its historic extreme it is anchored in Old Testament revelation. At its prophetic extreme it is anchored to that blessed hope, even the glorious appearing of our Lord Jesus Christ.

Its Scope

God's plan is great in its scope. How wide is it? "World-wide," the Bible answers. The Church must make disciples among all nations. Christ must be preached to every creature. The gospel must go to the uttermost part of the earth. "God so loved the world." Again, "The field is the world." Christ's command to go is found in each of the first five books in the New Testament. In the sixth book, and on through the Bible are repeated references to this enterprise. This is the work God has committed to his people. His plan moves through the confusion of our day, like the gulf stream through the ocean.

World evangelization is difficult, but not complicated. Gideon Ousley was a pioneer preacher of early Methodism. He tells that when he was called to preach he heard a voice speaking to him. The voice said, "Gideon, go preach my gospel."

Gideon answered, "Lord, I cannot, I am but a child."

The voice said, "Gideon, do you know the disease?"

"That I do, Lord," he said.

"Gideon, do you know the remedy?"

"I do, Lord," he answered.

The voice said, "Go tell them the disease and the remedy. The rest is nothing but chaff."

There is a divine simplicity about witnessing. In Argentina, enemies of the gospel have sought to ridicule us by saying, "They are crazy. They give people a bath and a book." What do these scoffers mean? They speak of baptism and the Bible. In reality, these words of ridicule are an apt summary. When a man believes, we baptize him and put a Bible in his hands. The essence of world evangelization is to win men to Christ, then build them into spiritual reproducers.

2. GEARING INTO GOD'S PLAN

Every Christian must fit into God's plan or miss life's meaning. We preachers often fail our listeners at this point. We present God's great program. Huge concepts! Vast horizons. But we fail to draw down-to-earth conclusions. Emotions are stirred and wills moved. But to what action? People are not told how to apply these matters to their lives. Frustration results. This need not be. World evangelization must be brought near.

Our text says, "Teach." Again it says, "Teaching." Those words are not the same. The first speaks of winning men to Christ. The second speaks of building men for Christ. "Teach" deals with evangelization, "teaching" with edification. Here world evangelization begins. Practical work faces every Christian. Start with this. Primitive Christians taught others of Christ and won them to Him. "Daily in the temple, and in every house, they ceased not to teach and preach Jesus Christ" (Acts 5:42). By teaching and preaching they led others to Jesus. In this way they filled the then known world with the gospel.

Getting Started

You have heard that crossing an ocean never made a missionary. That saying is true. Many people think that commitment to Christ means going to a foreign field. People who know they cannot go conclude they should do nothing. That is a mistake.

Commitment to Christ will make you face the world task. Witnessing begins where you are. Why offer to go elsewhere if you are not witnessing where you are? Let crossing the ocean be called step number five. Suppose you offer to take it. But you cannot. Why not? Because the only step you can take now is number one. Afterward comes number two. What is the first step? To teach someone how to be saved. Are you working at it? To take this step will ready you for whatever God has farther ahead for you. Abraham Lincoln said, "I will prepare myself. When my opportunity comes I will be ready."

You can only teach what you really know. Most Christians are reluctant to do personal work. When asked at the close of a service to help a seeking soul, Christians often say, "I cannot do personal work." Why not? Partly because you cannot teach what you do not know. Most Christians do not know how to use the Word of God to lead a soul to Christ. Therefore, you must read the Bible.

Perhaps you say, "I read my Bible." How do you read it? Daily? Ambitiously? According to some plan? Do you read from Genesis 1:1 to Revelation 22:21? Or are you content to read a Psalm or favorite chapter at bedtime?

Irregular reading of the word of God is more harmful than irregular eating. Have you ever thought how systematically you eat? Would a man be satisfied to eat only when his wife felt like cooking? Suppose she would skip a couple of days, then prepare a meal. Afterwards she might not cook again for several days.

A man would never submit to that! But think. Which life is more important, physical or spiritual? Your body will soon be food for worms. But the inner man will live forever. It is a tragedy to neglect regular Bible reading. Why not correct that error? Plan for daily, definite Bible reading. It may be one of the greatest things you have ever done.

Memorize Vital Texts

Daily memorizing and Bible reading have been the most blessed habits of my Christian life. Are you hiding Bible verses in your heart? God commands us to do so. And He promises to bless those who obey.

This I had to learn the hard way. I was converted when a freshman at the University of Nebraska. The next summer I went to Moody Institute in Chicago to study the Bible. When the registrar asked me what practical work I would do, I was not interested. I was confused and wanted someone to straighten me out. But the school authorities were firm. Every student had to do practical work. A choice was offered. Jail work, hospital work, or street work could be selected. I thought quickly. By eliminating the first two I decided on street work. There would be fresh air outdoors at least!

Failure

Came my first assignment. We piled into a station wagon and started south on Michigan Boulevard. We stopped in a Negro neighborhood. On the street corner we set up a small platform and folding organ. Our leader explained the plan. Certain group members were to give testimonies. We would sing hymns. Then he would begin to preach. When he began to preach, our duty was to speak to someone about Christ. What orders! If the leader had told me I was to be shot in five minutes I could hardly have felt worse! How the time fled by. It was the shortest meeting I was ever in. It seemed that in just a moment the leader was on the platform giving his message. The more experienced members of the group moved out and began to talk with individuals. There I stood rooted to the spot. I was scared stiff. But I knew I had to do something. I saw a man sitting in a nearby doorway, a big husky Negro. At least he was sitting down. I thought that was an advantage. So I moved slowly toward him. When I got near I said, "Good afternoon."

"Good afternoon," he said with a voice like the roar of a cannon.

I said, "Are you a Christian?"

"No," he said, with the same tremendous voice.

I said, "Would you like to be a Christian?"

"Yes," he said.

That was one of the biggest surprises of my life. When he said "yes," I felt like a person pushing hard against a shut door that suddenly gives way. I was thrown off balance. Unconsciously, of course, I was expecting a "no" answer. I had two or three weak little arguments. I am sure they would not have convinced a mosquito. But I was going to try them when the man said "no." Instead, he said "yes."

Crushed

I did not know what to do. Then I thought of my Bible. I opened it. The man sat there, eyes fixed intently on me. I turned hastily through the Bible. Not a single page seemed familiar. I went clear through the Old Testament, then the New Testament. I came to the end of the Bible. Then I decided to do like the Chinese. They read from back to front. So I went from Revelation to Genesis. Nothing! There I stood tongue-tied and helpless. I did not know what to do. Finally I said lamely, "The Lord bless you" and turned and walked away.

You may laugh, but it was no laughing matter to me. I got into that station wagon humbled and silent. If ever a fellow felt whipped, I did. Back at the institute, I climbed three flights of stairs in the old "153 building," went into my room, locked the door behind me, threw myself across the bed and cried like a baby. I said, "Oh, God, for the first time in my life I have been face to face with a man who wanted to become a Christian and I did not have even one Bible verse to show him the way." That night I promised God I would never again go out to witness without having learned chosen verses. A day or two later a fellow student started me memorizing Bible verses on cards.

I did not know then that God commands us to memorize His Word. He orders us to write His Word upon the table of our heart. Follow a plan for hiding God's Word in your heart. God will bless you in winning and building men.

3. GRASPING GOD'S PROMISE

Notice the condition and the promise. "Go, and lo I am with you all the days." This is the way to begin world evangelization. It is personal. Christ says, "You go, teach men of me. Win them. Build them in the faith." This is His command. The promise that goes with it is, "Lo, I am with you all the days." That is one of the greatest promises in the whole Bible. But the promise is conditioned on our obedience.

People sometimes claim promises while separating them from a condition on which they depend. That is not right. Only if we meet the condition can we claim the promise. Let us do what Jesus has commanded. Then He will fulfill the promise of His presence. How plainly our Lord puts it, "He that hath my commandments, and keepeth them, he it is that loveth me: and he that loveth me shall be loved of my Father, and I will love him, and will manifest myself to him." Obedience brings blessing. Take in God's Word daily in order to give it out each day. Win and build men for God. And Jesus Christ will go with you every day.

HIS MEAT, MY MEAT

"My meat is to do the will of him that sent me,
and to finish his work" (John 4:34).

Our Lord said this. How wonderful is His example. To be sure, unregenerate man can never do as he ought by self-effort. Thank God that in wondrous grace He shares His own life with the believer to supply necessary power! Still and all, apart from the indwelling life of Jesus, nothing so helps the Christian as the example of his Lord.

Every Christian should ask a question the Apostle Paul asked, "Lord, what wilt thou have me to do?" One answer our Lord gives is, "As my Father hath sent me, even so send I you" (John 20:21). God sent Jesus to perform a task. As He lived, we should live. The way He worked, we should work. Our mission is a projection of His mission. Let us note then, some things Jesus said about His work. And let us apply these truths to our own life.

1. "MY MEAT IS TO DO THE WILL OF HIM THAT SENT ME, AND TO FINISH HIS WORK"

This statement reminds us of a marksman getting on target. Jesus took aim. He planned the trajectory of His life. We should do the same. Jesus committed Himself to do God's work. God sent Him for this. The Greek noun meaning "work" also means "business." We will trace in John's Gospel what Jesus says about His relation to God's business. At the outset we see that Jesus purposed to finish God's business in the world.

This purpose squarely opposes the idea that Christianity is to make us comfortable. Materialism tends to make us self-centered and nearsighted. The materialist can only lay up treasures on earth. World evangelization urges men to lay up treasures in heaven. How sad it is when money in a sack is all a man has. In February, 1956, I was aboard a freighter in the Atlantic bound for Buenos Aires. Sam, a ship's officer, told me of a recent tragedy. The freighter was en route to Africa at the time. The steward was issuing new equipment to the crew. He ordered that the Chinese cook's worn-out mattress be replaced. A new mattress was issued. The old mattress was thrown overboard. When the cook returned to his cabin he asked where his mattress was. Crew members said, "We threw it overboard."

"My God!" was all he said. Then he told them his life savings, $10,000, were in the mattress. That night the Chinese cook threw himself overboard—a suicide. Someone says, "Poor fool!" Was he more a fool than the Christian who forfeits real riches for passing things?

Notice the verse which follows our text. Christ continues, "Say not ye, There are yet four months, and then cometh harvest? behold, I say unto you, Lift up your eyes, and look on the fields; for they are white already to harvest" (John 4:35). The whole context is missionary! The world is a harvest of souls. "Preach the gospel to every creature." This is the central thrust of the New Testament. This is what Christianity is about. God has placed us in the world to finish this business.

"On with the message, on with the light.
On to the regions still shrouded in night,
On to the nations that never have heard,
On with the life-giving, soul-saving Word."

2. "MY FATHER WORKETH HITHERTO, AND I WORK" (John 5:17)

What is the thought of this statement? Is it not to work with God? Jesus was working with God toward a common goal. Every Christian should know he is doing the same. What an anchor this is in an hour of crisis. This is the assurance we need in these perilous days when the world is out of joint. It is wonderful to work for God. It is even better to know we are working with God in the task of His choice. The Christian is not asked to try something, then seek God's blessing upon it. No indeed. The question is, what is God doing in our day? The Bible says God will get the gospel to the ends of the earth. He will do this through Christians. "We are labourers together with God," wrote Paul.

United in Purpose

This makes identification with Christ practical. Christians should be identified with both the person and purpose of Christ. Jesus said, "I am the vine, ye are the branches" (John 15:5). Again, "If ye abide in me" (John 15:7). And again, "I in them" (John

17:23). We are united to the Lord Jesus that we may with Him bear the gospel to the ends of the earth. This truth makes life meaningful. And death loses its terror. Moravian missionaries had a noble emblem. It shows an ox standing between a plow and an altar. Underneath are the words, "Ready for Either." The plow represents service, the altar, sacrifice. The Christian should be ready to live or die for Christ.

Missionary Golaz and his young wife died within a year after reaching Senegambia in Africa. To the friend that wiped the death damp from his brow Golaz said, "Tell the Church not to be discouraged if the first laborers fall in the field. Their graves will mark the way for their successors who will march past them with great strides." Golaz knew he was moving with God toward God's goal. That fact consoled him. How else can a man say in his last hour, "O death where is thy sting? O grave where is thy victory?"

3. "THIS IS THE WORK OF GOD, THAT YE BELIEVE ON HIM WHOM HE HATH SENT" (John 6:29)

God's business is bound up with faith in Christ. A man had asked Jesus the question, "What shall we do that we might work the works of God?" In other words, "What does it mean to do God's business?" The answer, "Vital faith in Christ." His "you go" can hardly be obeyed without faith. And only faith that issues in obedience is real. Faith's touchstone is obedience. John Wesley said, "Pray like all depended on God. Work like all depended on you."

We may know about faith, yet not believe. We

may read that "faith is the substance of things hoped for" (Heb. 11:1). We may understand that "without faith it is impossible to please him" (Heb. 11:6). But to know this does not gear a man into the missionary task. We may admire Abraham the father of the faithful. We may be thrilled at the fact that "he staggered not at the promise of God through unbelief" (Rom. 4:20). But admiration for Abraham is not obedience to Christ's command, "Go ye." So our Lord clearly implies, "Do you really believe in me? Then, obey me."

"Obedient Unto Death"

Faith and obedience sent the late Rowland Bingham and two companions far into Africa to open the work that is today the Sudan Interior Mission. Dr. Bingham says, "With still further supplies, I followed my two companions up as far as I could go and still keep communication with the coast. There the news finally filtered through that both of my companions had laid down their lives. Since there was no Board at home to send on reinforcements or to act for me in any way, five months after their death I decided to return to see what could be done to arouse interest in the great Sudan and to form a responsible Board. Upon my return the whole expedition was written down as a failure. What was there to show for the effort? Nothing but two graves. I visited Mrs. Gowans, Walter's mother, to take to her the few personal belongings of her son. As I was shown into her parlor, she met me with extended hand. We stood there with hands clasped in silence for a while. Then she said these words that I shall never forget, 'Well Mr. Bingham, I would rather have had Walter go out to the Sudan and die there, all alone, than have him home today, disobeying his Lord.' " A mother's confidence in Christ and two lives laid down! This is the faith and obedience that will finish world evangelization.

4. "I MUST WORK THE WORKS OF HIM THAT SENT ME, WHILE IT IS DAY: THE NIGHT COMETH WHEN NO MAN CAN WORK" (John 9:4)

The task is urgent. Night comes. As Jeremiah said, "Alas! for the day declines, the evening shadows lengthen" (Jer. 6:4, Amplified). Every day we delay the gospel's outgoing, eternal night swallows thousands of unreached souls. Time, like a flood, bears all the sons of men away.

One of the most touching prefaces in any book is that by K. S. Lee, a Chinese Christian. It says, "These pages are dedicated to the memory of my mother who during all her life could neither read nor write one word, and who never traveled more than 10 miles from her birthplace. Born in a pagan environment, she died without Christian faith. Whose sin was this? 'For . . . how shall they believe in him of whom they have not heard? and how shall they hear without a preacher? And how shall they preach, except they be sent?' There are millions of mothers all over the world today, born in pagan homes, who will die without knowledge of the true God unless you and I do our part. Whose sin is this?"

Shadows Lengthen

"The night cometh." What else can it mean? Night shades of sin advance across the world? Think of

110

the words, "Thirty million slain." This horrible news from red China came over the teletypes of the world. Communist leaders announced that during the past ten years thirty million Chinese had been liquidated. Among these were "people who refused to renounce Christianity." The staggering weight of agony caused by Communism would crush us could we know it. We may selfishly reason that we, at least, are safe. Are we?

Communists declare they expect to dominate America by 1966 and the world by 1970. They have already fulfilled 42 per cent of their program in the U.S.A. Khrushchev boasts that war with America will be unnecessary because Communist infiltration will cause our country to fall "like an overripe fruit falls from a tree." A Communist source states that 50,000,000 Americans will be killed if their plan is carried out. Imagine, a newspaper headline, "Fifty Million Americans Killed." Will that news flash around the world within 10 years? We do not know. We do know that Jesus said, "I must work . . . the night cometh . . ." To evangelize the world is urgent!

5. "FATHER ... I HAVE FINISHED THE WORK WHICH THOU GAVEST ME TO DO" (John 17:4)

This was Jesus' prayer in the shadow of the cross. Jesus had determined from the first to finish God's business. He had let nothing turn Him aside. If the Church is to evangelize the world we must pinpoint our objectives. We must sharply focus on work yet to be done. Not all Christians work is of equal value. Some activities must be pruned.

Every Christian should cut away from his life things unessential. Pruning is not pleasant. But new life vitalizes parts which remain, once useless branches are gone. Christians are cumbered with many things. "Much serving" is our problem, as it was Martha's. To finish God's business we must make our strokes count. Paul said, "This one thing I do."

General Ulysses Grant conquered General Lee, won the Civil War, and became President of the United States. But during his last years he got into Wall Street and fell into the hands of crooks. Grant's good name was used to cheat the public out of $16,000,000. At last the crash came. Overwhelmed by debts, Grant handed over his farm, his houses in Philadelphia and New York, even his trophies and swords. Grant was bankrupt and dying of cancer. But he still had a goal. He knew that when he was dead his widow would be poverty stricken. Therefore, to provide for her, he decided to write his memoirs. He dictated until the cancer in his throat got so bad he could not speak. He scribbled the last of the book in pencil, while he suffered agony. Grant did the last chapter just three days before he died. The book was published and paid Mrs. Grant almost half a million dollars in royalties.

Let each ask himself: Am I working for world evangelization? Have I pinpointed my goals? Am I pressing toward them with like determination?

6. "IT IS FINISHED" (John 19:30)

This was Christ's triumphant cry from the cross. His victory belongs to every Christian. It is part of our birthright. This is basic as we commit ourselves to Christ to finish God's business. Death cannot thwart God's plan. Each of us must face death, unless Christ comes first. But death itself is softened by the certainty that ultimate victory is ours in the missionary task.

Adoniram Judson labored for 32 years in Burma before taking a furlough. He took one then to save his wife's life. All the time he was home on furlough his heart was in Burma. He was so delighted with that far-off field of labor that he said he would not leave Burma to be made king of the greatest empire on earth. Judson suffered innumerable hardships. But he said he would rather die than give up his work for the Burmans. This is what he wrote,

"One prayer, my God, thy will be done,
One only good I crave;
To finish well my work,—and rest
Within a Burman grave."

I cannot conclude without pressing the personal question upon you. It alone matters. Are you fully yielded to Christ, actively doing His work? World evangelization is His will for our age.

Step Forward

Garibaldi, the great Italian patriot, during Italy's war for independence challenged his soldiers with these words, "I am going out from Rome. I offer neither quarters nor provisions nor wages. I offer hunger, thirst, forced marches, battles, and death. Let him who loves me with his heart, and not with his lips only, follow me." History records that every one of Garibaldi's soldiers stepped forward. Christ says today, "I am going out. I offer neither quarters nor provisions, nor wages. I offer hunger, thirst, forced marches, battles, and death. Let him who loves me with his heart, and not with his lips only, follow me." Will you step forward? You will never regret having given yourself to Jesus Christ for this work. Make it your meat to do God's will, to finish His business.

FINISH THE VITAL TASK

"Yea, so have I strived to preach the gospel, not where Christ was named, lest I should build upon another man's foundation: But as it is written, To whom he was not spoken of, they shall see: and they that have not heard shall understand" (Rom. 15:20,21).

1. DIRECTION: "NOT WHERE CHRIST WAS NAMED"

This phrase reveals an underlying principle of Paul's ministry. Paul was committed to the task of reaching people who had not yet heard the gospel message. This basic pattern could easily be missed by a casual reader of Paul's writings. But in our text the great apostle speaks very plainly. He declares that the thrust of his witness had always been toward areas where "Christ's name had never been mentioned." "But [instead I would act on the principle], as it is written, they shall see who have never been told of Him, and they shall understand who have never heard [of Him]" (Rom. 15:21, Amplified).

Paul got this plan from God. God has a goal. Divine revelation tells man God's goal. In other words, the Bible reveals God's program. This fact is important. It is personal. It is intensely practical.

Two Questions

Here is a lost man. He is convicted of sin and longs to be saved. To do that he must find out who Jesus Christ is and surrender his life to Him. Afterward he must obey Jesus Christ. We see this pattern in the conversion of Saul of Tarsus, later Paul. God's bright light strikes Paul down in the dust of the Damascus road. There, in a moment of time, Paul's world falls apart. He finds out he has been completely mistaken in the deepest convictions of his life. Then he asks two significant questions. First, "Who art thou, Lord?" (Acts 9:5). On the identity of Jesus hinges the salvation of Paul's soul, and that of every man and woman on earth.

Paul's second question is, "Lord, what wilt thou have me to do?" The answer to that question will determine the whole course of Paul's life. And so it will for each of us. Paul declares Jesus said to him, "I have appeared unto thee for this purpose, to make thee a minister and a witness . . . Delivering thee from the people, and from the Gentiles, unto whom now I send thee, To open their eyes, and to turn them from darkness to light, and from the power of Satan unto God, that they may receive forgiveness of sins . . ." (Acts 26:16-18).

There we see God's plan to evangelize the world. God does not say all men are to be saved. God does say the Church must offer every man that opportunity. That is evangelization. Christian, anchor your life to Christ for this. Sink your roots down into the purpose of God for this age.

Things Pass Away

It is folly to seek happiness in material things.

Men who do that see their castles go to pieces like soap bubbles grasped with the hand. If you try to make money for money's sake you will pierce yourself with many sorrows. The Bible says that. Your own ambition can be a deadly thing. Deal at the cross with your stubborn determination to have your own way. To dedicate your life to a program that is not God's is to waste it. No human life lived at cross purposes with God's plan can have God's blessing.

Thousands of men and women today are being duped into thinking their well-being lies in material things. They are lured by the glitter of boats, cars, appliances, gadgets, and lovely homes. How easily the heart can become occupied with things. But material benefits are not permanent. They will cheat your soul at last. No man is smart who lives primarily for this world. "For all that is in the world, the lust of the flesh, and the lust of the eyes, and the pride of life, is not of the Father, but is of the world. And the world passeth away, and the lust thereof . . ." (I John 2:16,17).

A Sure Anchor

These issues are real to me. Many men have better brains than mine. Thousands are more talented. But years ago I saw clearly that world evangelization is the purpose of God for our age. That is what God is doing. That is the task nearest His heart. I committed myself to Jesus Christ to help with that job.

As years have passed the way has not always been easy. The mission field has its peculiar discouragements. Times of depression are like deep, dark valleys. But one fact has anchored my soul. It is this. My life belongs to Jesus Christ for world missions.

And that enterprise is first in God's plan for our age. I urge you to commit yourself to God. You will never regret having anchored your life to Christ. Give yourself to Him to do His will in world evangelization.

2. DETERMINATION: "STRIVED . . . GOSPEL"

The gospel is God's unique message. The whole Bible is not the gospel. To tell people to keep the ten commandments is not the gospel. To practice the golden rule is not the gospel. To join a church and be confirmed or baptized and partake of the Lord's supper is not the gospel. What is the gospel anyway?

The Apostle Paul wrote, "I declare to you the gospel which I preached unto you . . . that Christ died for our sins according to the scriptures; And that he was buried, and that he rose again the third day according to the scriptures" (I Cor. 15:1,3,4). In reality Jesus Christ himself is offered to man. The gospel is Christ offered to man in terms of what He has done for man.

This good news is supremely important to all men everywhere. Christ alone offers man eternal life. All men enter the world spiritually dead because of sin. Christ came "to seek and to save that which was lost" (Luke 19:10). Nothing is so vital to unreached men as for them to hear the gospel. It offers them life.

Hard at It

"I have strived to preach the gospel," says Paul. God's number one job deserves man's number one effort. Nathan Hale of Revolutionary War fame died as a spy. His patriotic words were, "My only regret is that I have but one life to give for my country." No man or woman has more. One life to invest! Will you give it to God? Give it with abandon. Live to make your strokes count for world evangelization.

Raymond Lull lived and died like that. He witnessed for God among the Muslems. They drove him away. When almost eighty he returned once more to Arabia to tell of Christ's love. In fury the Muslems dragged him outside the city and stoned him to death. So died Raymond Lull, striving to preach the gospel where Christ was not named. God grant us whole-heartedness like that!

Jim Elliot was one of the five martrys in Ecuador. Jim said, "Live so that when you come to die, you will have nothing to do but die." World missions is God's program for today. Study the facts. Be convinced of them. Then commit yourself to Christ. Ask Him to make your life, influence, money, prayers, count in that job. That alone matters.

Paul's Passion

No example is more stirring than Paul's own. "Strive" reveals Paul's earnestness in the missionary task. In that word is wrapped up toil, persecution, sufferings, anguish, sweat, and blood. Paul's passion was to get the gospel to the world. He lived for nothing else. He had no other capital. He said, "As sorrowful, yet alway rejoicing; as poor, yet making many rich; as having nothing, and yet possessing all things" (II Cor. 6:10). Again he said, "I am debtor both to the Greeks, and to the Barbarians; both to the wise, and to the unwise" (Rom. 1:14).

Acts 20 shows Paul pouring himself out to evangelize Ephesus. Three years pass. He must leave. With the church elders Paul reviews the record. He tells of his tears and temptation, how he kept back nothing profitable to them, how he taught publicly and from house to house. Paul says he doesn't know what the future holds except for the Holy Spirit's witness that bonds and afflictions await him. That might have stopped a lesser man. Not so Paul. He says, "But none of these things move me, neither count I my life dear unto myself, so that I might finish my course with joy, and the ministry, which I have received of the Lord Jesus, to testify the gospel of the grace of God" (Acts 20:24). Paul strove mightily through all his life to reach the unreached for Christ.

3. DECISION: "I," A PERSONAL MATTER

Life's great decisions are made alone. Here Paul uses the first person singular pronoun "I." He does not invoke the decision of a committee. He does not say he was carrying out the plan of his local church. Much less was he voicing a denominational program. Paul had wrestled and prayed this matter through for himself. He understood God's purpose to evangelize the world. By God's grace he determined to do his part. Every Christian ought to do the same.

Men Who Dared

Joshua, you may recall, set a good example. He had led the children of Israel for many years. But he saw that their hearts were turning away from God. So Joshua hurled a challenge in the teeth of the whole crowd. He said, "And if it seem evil unto you to serve the Lord, choose you this day whom ye will serve . . . but as for me and my house, we will serve the Lord" (Josh. 24:15).

Luther had his lonely decision to make. We see him at last before the Diet of Worms. The great hall is packed. The humble servant of the Lord is surrounded with the might, splendor, and pomp of Europe. Most of the men present are thirsting for Luther's blood. This is no time to invoke decisions of committees. There Luther stands, apparently a helpless man. But in the deep loneliness of his own heart-searching before God, Luther had made his choice. And the immortal words ring out to echo down the ages: "It is neither safe nor right to go against conscience, for my conscience is captive to God's Word alone. Here I take my stand. So help me God, I can do no other."

Question Is Clear

Notice the exact nature of Paul's decision. Paul lived to evangelize the world. And what of us? Must we not reach the lost of our generation who have never heard of Christ? That means to concentrate on the unfinished task. It means to give men and money to reach the unreached. Let those who will talk of home needs. We have no quarrel with them. The gospel witness is valuable wherever given. But those who see God's plan will put the unreached first. They must have priority.

Gospel-wise the world is divided into two classes of people. There are those who can hear the gospel, and those who cannot. Our job is to reach for Christ those who cannot hear. Consider this carefully. The good may be the enemy of the best. Let no lesser need, however attractive, bar you from God's best.

By God's grace help reach the unreached. Pray constantly for the completion of world evangelization. By faith claim the parts of the world not yet evangelized.

Cross the Line

This is a great issue. A line has been drawn. Beyond it stand Christians who are committed to Christ for world evangelization. Are you willing to cross the line? Captain Francisco Pizarro was the conqueror of Peru. The hardships of his first two expeditions filled ten long years. The first expedition of almost 200 men returned without reaching Peru. One soldier out of every four had died. Nonetheless, a new expedition was launched in the year 1526. Again began the fight with adversity. The heat of the desert, then stinking swamps and jungles were followed by the bitter cold of mountain peaks. The constant attacks of savage Indians took their toll.

The governor of Panama, exasperated by the loss of so many lives, resolved to recall the expedition. He sent two ships to the island where Pizarro had his camp, with orders to return. Pizarro's men received the ships with demonstrations of wildest joy. Only one thought prevailed once hunger was satisfied. That was to turn back and forget Peru forever. But the same vessels brought Pizarro letters. The letters told him not to give up hope. Elements needed to go forward would soon come.

That was all the Spanish captain needed. One ray of hope! He prepared once more the most desperate assault imaginable. With firm voice he announced his purpose. "Pizarro drew his dagger," says a writer, "and with evident determination marked a line from east to west. Then with a gesture toward the south where he had suffered such misery he said, 'Friends and comrades, this is the side of death, hardships, hunger, nakedness, storms, and abandonment. The other side is that of pleasure. To the north you may go to Panama to be poor. To the south to Peru to be rich. Let every good Spaniard choose which suits him best.' " Adding that, as for himself, he would go to the south, he crossed the line. He was followed by thirteen men. One of the boats immediately turned its prow toward Panama bearing the quitters. Pizarro took possession of the other boat. With but thirteen brave men he set sail for Peru. That decision changed the course of history.

Will you cross the line? God asks your yielded life for His work. Will you be faithful unto death? Or until the last man or woman is reached? Souls must be won from every kindred, tongue, people, and nation. You can cross the line even now.

When you are finished with this book, why not pass it on to a friend?

A MISSIONARY CANTATA!

THE GREATEST STORY YET UNTOLD

Are you acquainted with "The Greatest Story Yet Untold," a unique, all-season missionary cantata composed and arranged by Eugene L. Clark of Back to the Bible Broadcast? The challenge to world evangelization is presented dramatically and effectively through excellent arrangements of both old and new missionary songs of merit. The music is strengthened by interwoven scriptural narrative.

"The Greatest Story Yet Untold" is appealing to both the professional choir and the average volunteer choir, whose rehearsal time and musical training are usually limited. A must for your church!

$1.25 each, or 12 or more copies at $1.00 each*

BACK TO THE BIBLE BROADCAST
Box 233 ● Lincoln 1, Nebraska / or Box 10 ● Winnipeg, Manitoba

* U.S. or Canadian Currency